MW01182014

IMAGINE THE POWER

Getting to Success Faster

By

Terah Stearns

ISBN: 1-4107-7160-1 (e-book)
ISBN: 1-4107-7161-X (Paperback)
ISBN: 1-4107-7162-8 (Dust Jacket)

This book is printed on acid free paper.

1stBooks – rev. 08/29/03

Dedication

With great respect and great love, I dedicate this book to my husband, Lloyd Stearns; to my father and mother, Pat and Betty Duncan, and to that wonderful individual who first said, "Yes, I'll hire you."

To my husband, Lloyd, who has never stopped believing in me; who has championed everything I have ever done, no matter how scary. I thank you for your unconditional love and support.

To my father, Pat Duncan, who never let me rest on my laurels, who challenged even a 95 on a test because he knew I could be better. I thank you for your amazing love and support.

To my mother, Betty Duncan, for her absolute belief and wonder in my accomplishments, who complimented me when I was unsure and bragged about me even when I didn't think I deserved it.

To those thousands of individuals who supported my belief that we could succeed together and played guinea pig to my developing leadership skills. To all those who listened as I developed new ideas and were willing to let go of the rocks and barriers long enough to see if we really could swim!

To you, my dear readers, who bought this book believing in your future and what I had to offer. You have my heart and my blessing, my belief in you and my conviction that you can succeed if you can *imagine the power* within each of us and honor it each and everyday.

Acknowledgements

No book is ever published without enormous support. This book is no exception. I have known for a long time that I would write a book. I just kept wondering what I had to say. Over the years, people have spoken highly of my methods but I wasn't always sure that I could tell anyone what it was I did. For years it just felt like magic!

In 2002, I began to write down my thoughts to support my coaching and consulting clients through various pieces of their process. The notes began to take form and the feedback from these people kept coming back, "You should put this in a book!" So I began to collect them and built a table of contents that seemed to have some substance.

The power of intention is such that within a few weeks, I was a keynote speaker at a wonderful convention hosted by Sophie Konuwa, Director of Small Business Development at Butte College in Chico, California. It was a wonderful group of female entrepreneurs and in the audience was a publisher, Leslie Gilbertie. Leslie asked to me if I had considered putting my thoughts in a book... voila! Intention = Result!

I was committed and as Goethe said (highly paraphrased) once you commit the universe opens up more possibilities than you can imagine. The book began to flow.

My wonderful colleague, Bob Hawkins at http://www.hawkconsulting.com helped edit the book and shared ideas for titles.

The funniest part is that while the material flowed easily the title refused to appear! This amazing work has had more titles than names in a phonebook. Wonderful friends, like Doug Whatley at http://www.sp3group.com and Laurel Barton at http://www.oswegoconsulting.com offered brainstorming and suggestions, many of which ended up on the title page for a while. All were good but nothing made my toes tingle (a sure sign of alignment!)

Finally, as I typed the last line of the last chapter, I knew I had to have the title. No little pressure because you can't go to print until you have the title. The book is ready, the title… I finished the book sitting in the Admiral's Club at the Austin-Bergstrom International Airport (my home away from home.) I climbed on my American flight and became engaged with two delightful ladies, one of whom was a graduate student in advertising at the University of Texas.

I began to explain that the book was done and I even knew what picture I wanted on the cover. She asked me what the last sentence I had typed was. I told her it was about imagining the power of working together rather than working in resistance. She smiled at me and said, "There's your title…Imagine the Power." My toes tingled!

So now we have a title, cover art, and content. Now all we are waiting for is *you*…to turn the page and *Imagine the Power!*

Table of Contents

Introduction

Success…you can get there from here. No matter where you are, you can get there. The issue is how attached you are to *how* you get there.

Cryptic sentence, right? The fact is that within every organization, within every person, there is amazing potential. Unfortunately, our society and the systems we have built don't allow much room for that potential. Our very active self-talk doesn't allow much support for it either. But it's there. It will rock your world when you learn how to really tap into it and create better outcomes.

This book is a manual to help any person and any organization create that success. Each chapter is built around a specific topic. Each topic is offered with steps to unleash that potential. ***This manual is unlike any management or leadership book you have ever read because it tells you HOW to do what you need to do to create the success you want and tap into the amazing power within your organization.*** While the concepts and principles of leadership are clearly within the pages of this handbook ***I go one step*** further and tell you *HOW to* do them.

This book offers you the questions, the process, the sequence, the intention and much more that you will need to begin plumbing the creativity and excellence of your organization.

Whether you are a manager, executive, or business owner you will find this book supportive of your success. If you are a team lead or a team member these techniques will help you be more powerful in your day to day interactions. You will be seen as a leader which is always helpful in any endeavor (and great for promotions!)

This handbook has been written with simplicity and I have done my best to capture the feeling that this is a *coaching session*. It has a personal one-on-one feeling that I believe you will find supports your questions and process.

We have all experienced the power of negativity and resistance in organizations. ***Imagine the power*** if all that energy were shifted instead to success mode!

It actually takes more energy to resist something than it does to move with it. Think about that for a moment. *Imagine* you are trying to swim against the rapids. Feel how much energy it takes to swim against the white water. Now… *imagine that you relax and begin to flow with the current, making small course corrections with minimal effort.* It seems effortless, doesn't it? But how often in the course of our day do we resist and fight what's happening. *Imagine* what would happen if you had the *tools* to effectively let go and still create the right outcomes…to *flow* with the course of events. *Imagine* what would happen if you not only made these course corrections but had a team <u>rowing</u> with you! *Imagine* how swiftly change and success could come to you.

Negativity is a huge power drain. Think of the times when you have felt most negative. Weren't you tired? It takes amazing energy to be and stay negative. Stay there long enough and you will experience depression. Stay there longer and you will not have enough oomph to get out of bed!

I'm not talking about esoteric nonsense here. I'm talking the realm of possibility. No matter how bad it may be within your organization, you can make these shifts. In the course of my twenty five years in business, I have become an expert in helping organizations turn around. I have helped 17 organizations go from bust to boom. Each of these organizations has been in diverse industries and markets. Over 25 years, we have been in good and bad economies. There was little commonality in the structure or leadership of any of these organizations.

There was only one common denominator for all of these groups…they were made up of <u>*people*</u>. No business or organization can be created or survive without people. People make the business on the inside and the outside. If you don't have the balance of skills to manage and lead, the hard and the soft skills, the process and the intention, you will find yourself struggling against the current of negativity. Bring the skills into alignment and balance and you'll be flying over the water! *Imagine the power! Imagine the exhilaration! Imagine the joy and energy with which you could meet each opportunity.*

In over 25 years, people have never failed to surprise me with their gifts and talents, their creativity and enthusiasm, and their joy at being respected and heard. You too, can enjoy this feeling and the great part of the excursion…you won't be alone. Because _together_ we succeed! Imagine the power and rejoice in your potential!

With great respect,

Terah

Prologue

How to Use this Book

Here it is! The information you've been waiting for. This book has been designed to help you do the job you need to do step by step. Do you need to communicate more effectively? Go to Chapter 9. There step by step I'll lead you through powerful communication skills and tools with examples and stories to help you integrate the skills.

Do you need to get better performance from your staff? Chapters 1, 3, 11, 12 and 13 are all geared toward the various steps to getting excellent performance from your direct reports.

Do you have to fire someone and are concerned as to how to do it well and not lose your courage and all your sleep? Chapter 13 shows you the four steps and hopefully saves you the trouble of having to fire them because you get the performance you need by following steps 1 and 2 so effectively! If you have to fire them, then you have a personal lesson plan on what to say and not to say, who should be involved and what to watch out for.

Do you need to manage a diverse group and need help making them work effectively together? Chapters 2, 3 and 14 will help you get results quickly!

Each chapter has the *Basics, Intention, and full Structure and Process* to effectively and effortlessly manage the situation. Then you'll have an example or integration scenario to put all the pieces together.

I've created a *how-to* manual that will guide every step of the way and be your own private executive coach in dealing with the leadership challenges and people management issues we all face from day to day.

Chapter 1

Setting Expectations

Setting expectations with employees is a critical success factor (CSF) in running a strong organization with passion and purpose. It is also a CSF in helping you enjoy your job and working effectively with your people. If expectations are set clearly, clarified and confirmed on both sides, you will find it easier to do the rest of your job, from performance appraisals to final project close-out and even, heaven forbid, to firing people. You will find that this process will set the stage for almost all future conversations with your staff and help you manage up, down and sideways!

The Basics

Being effective in this process means getting clear on what you are attempting to do. Understand that everyone has strengths and weaknesses. When you focus on a successful outcome you will get further than with disciplinary actions

15

(getting tough.) Setting a picture for success will help you and your teams perform with more strength and flexibility. Managers will frequently tell me "I just want to make everyone behave and act like professionals." Now, that would be a wonderful outcome but not everyone will visualize the same behavior and actions so your results will be variable at best.

I'm sure you are asking yourself, why *isn't* that a good outcome? Consider this, while you have an excellent work ethic, you may also have the critical thinking skills to see a larger picture or you will have more information because of your position. Therefore YOU *know* why people must play together effectively. YOU know what jobs need to be done, by whom and why. YOU know what communication should be happening by and with whom and why. That's wonderful. **Now, consider this: *your people don't know what you know!*** Assume nothing. What you take for granted, others have not even considered. This may surprise you but it is very true.

Now, you are probably saying, "but I've told them what to do and with whom." Yes, you've told them. But when working with people *telling doesn't work!* Think back to a time when you were going through a big change or had to do something you weren't sure how to do. If someone came in, told you what to do and then left, how effective were you?

Now if you were in the top 20% of your organization you followed several courses:
1. You found an expert, coach or mentor.

2. You found your boss and persisted in getting information you needed.
3. You hacked your way through the process and treated each new success with a sense of accomplishment.

Now if you were in the middle 70% of your organization, you followed a few of these ideas:
1. You asked questions of others or observed what they were doing but didn't want to ruffle anyone.
2. You patiently tried various things until one worked but tended to get frustrated with the process.
3. You did a little of both and prayed you wouldn't get in trouble.

Now if you performing in the bottom 10% of your organization:
1. You got angry.
2. You put down the system, the process, and/or the people who should have trained you.
3. You just didn't try and had a hundred excuses when someone asked for results.
4. And more than likely you slowed everyone else down in the system complaining angrily about what should , be done (but you weren't doing!)

These are pretty typical responses and you could probably add even more. What's important is to realize these styles, begin helping people integrate faster into the system, and acknowledge what you need to do as a leader.

We as managers/leaders make too many assumptions in this regard and then chant the mantra, "Why don't these people get it?" So the question for you is: WHERE are they going to get it? From you? You bet!

People will often say, "Leaders are the ones with the vision, purpose, mission, etc." what they are really saying is…*you're the one with the map of the world, tell us where the heck we're going and what you want me to do to help!*

Enlightening, isn't it? You bet. And how much of this big picture, charting the course, role definition, etc. do we really do? Not much and not well. In every organization where I have consulted, especially in times of turmoil, in each and every one of them, the majority of the staff was completely ignorant of the "big picture." Not just the overview but the real, clear picture; the "WHAT"; fully defined.

Every time we started drawing on the walls and laying out the map, they got it and ran with it! So let's keep the intention, if our folks are working and playing well together, it's more *not* just *their professionalism* that's active but *their knowledge* of where we're going, why and how they can help!

Will you get them all on board at once? Probably not. Some are slower than others or learn in different ways. Some have never been challenged to think critically. But if you hold the intention that they can do what's needed. They can support the greater good. They can work and play well together. IF you build the right picture and communicate it well…then you will be a hero and your people will blow your socks off!

The Intention

The key here is to focus on the belief that everyone really does want to do a good job, however, they may not see that what they do affects others or what the real outcome should be. They are just doing their job as they've determined it needs to be done. When they understand this big picture and their part in it you can begin to hold them accountable and have more relevant conversations around improving process and delivery.

Session Structure and Process

This method is effective whether someone has worked in your area for a long time or is newly arrived. You may have to set the context for the discussion differently depending on their status but the message is the same.

The context for the meeting is to establish what they think the organization is in business to do and how they play a role in a positive outcome. The technique for this conversation is set below.

Pre-session Planning

- You'll be looking at your organization as two groups: the proven performers and those that need to pick up the pace. The first step is to consider who on your team is doing an excellent job. This allows you to gather some positive feedback for further conversations. Before you meet with your best workers to ask yourself these questions and then as you interview your top performers you will have more to work with as you set expectations for others.

19

- o In the context of your organization's delivery: What does success look like to you?
- o Where do you see problems in the service and delivery of your department?
- o What would you like to see done better, more often or differently?
- o Now thinking of your top 20% performers : How do they view themselves in the organization? What's your view of their view?
- o What makes them successful in your eyes?
- o What do they do that others don't?
- o Why do they take these extra steps?

- When you understand what makes your excellent performers tick then it will be easier to see where others are off track. You can also see gaps in your process thinking.
- The next step will be to carry these conversations to the rest of your staff to gain their view and reset any perceptions that are off track. We'll go into more detail shortly.
- The questions you will want to consider for the second group are:
  - o How do they view themselves in the organization?
  - o What do they see as the most important part of their role?
  - o Who is their customer in their eyes?
  - o What do they think success looks like?
  - o What would they like to do but don't feel they have the authority or confidence to do?

o What would help them do the above? (IF it's what you would like them to do!)

Session Opening

Meet with your staff individually beginning as suggested with your top 20%. Let each know that this is just to evaluate if the organization is on the right track and where it can be improved. At this stage have no intention to resolve major performance issues. You are gaining insights and having discussions to help reset expectations. Use the questions above to help guide the conversation.

Explain the process of working together

Let your staff know when you find a misperception. Do this in a friendly conversational manner. Ask them how they have handled issues similar to the problems you identified in your analysis of the organization.

Note: Don't do too much set up for the problem. What you are looking for in this conversation is an understanding of how they think through the process of the business outcomes.

Example:
Manager: John, one of the problems that sometimes crosses my desk is customer complaints about late shipping. The customer has been told to expect their order by Thursday and it hasn't even been shipped by Thursday. What would you do to handle this call? (Wait for answer.) What do you think created this problem? (Wait for answer.) What would you do to change the process? (Wait for answer.) How do you think this improvement would affect the company? (Wait for answer.)

21

What takes place in these conversations is:
1. A greater understanding for the employee of the consequences of various daily activities. *If I see this, something else might happen or be improved.* For instance when you ask the question about how the change might impact the company listen for understanding of cause and effect. Do they see their job as important to the company?
2. A greater understanding for you of how the employee sees their job.
3. A chance to begin resetting their perceptions.

What you will do as they answer all of these questions is share your thoughts on what you would like to see. Be careful not to make the employee feel wrong and use effective communications styles. We'll spend more time on some of those styles in a later chapter.

Some ways to respond to answers that don't hit the mark or could have negative consequences can be:
- I appreciate what you are saying and I believe what would help the customer even more would be...
- I can see how you might come to that conclusion. I would suggest in the future trying...
- Or – That's an interesting idea, what else might be even more effective from the customer's view point.

After giving this feedback ask them why *they think you* would prefer this new approach. Again, you are trying to get them to evaluate using different criteria and see the big picture. Don't hesitate to ask them what impact this new suggestion might have on the company (even if all they see is the consequence to the next department.)

- Consistently ask the employee what the impact is on the organization, department, or customer.
- If they do not understand the depth of the situation, ask them to step into the customer's shoes or yours sharing what may be perceived from the other side.
- Ask them if they were running the operation, what would they expect? What would success look like for this department if they were the CEO?

Rules and Tools: Use active learning tools

Experiential activities, such as opportunities to practice applying concepts, interaction with manager on specific topics, hands-on demonstrations, role plays, etc. all stimulate the employee to participate actively, rather than listening passively to the conversation.

Adult learning research shows that adults prefer to learn by validating information based on experiences rather than simply accepting concepts at face value. It takes more preparation to have a session with good experiential learning exercises, but if you are interested in having employees develop a deep understanding of the business or subject, it is worth the effort.

Focus the discussion

While these conversations can take time out of your day, they are powerful and will set your course for more success later. However it is critical to keep the conversation focused. Be prepared with your questions and when the conversation drifts to other topics, make note of their questions or concerns but politely let them know you want to stick with the agenda/topic. Some people love to throw in a lot of other internal or external departmental issues. Thank them, make a note of their idea and then bring them back to topic.

In a later lesson we will look at various communication methods in depth but a quick one that will support this process is to use clarifying and confirming. This technique helps keep the person on track and makes sure that you have got the right picture.

When you clarify, you are asking for more information. When you confirm, you are restating what you heard and getting their agreement. You will find that this simple technique will reveal invaluable clarity about the way they think and feel about the organization.

Example:
Manager: Tell me about your current process for filling orders.
Employee: Well, I... (employee expresses process.)
Manager: What do you do when you find parts out of stock that delay orders? (A problem the manager had previously identified.) (Clarifying)
Employee: Usually, I make a note of it on my pocket pad and put it on the daily report.
Manager: What do you do with the daily report? (Clarifying)

Employee: Well, I put it in Daisy's inbox at the end of my shift.

Manager: So you keep detailed notes throughout the day and then create your daily report from those notes. Then turn them into Daisy at the end of the shift. **(Confirming)**

Employee: Sure, yeah, is that wrong?

Manager: No, nothing's wrong. I'm just wondering what does Daisy do when you hand them in?

Employee: I don't know, she's usually not there when my shift ends.

Manager: Does Daisy have a special box for these daily reports? **(Clarifying)**

Employee: No, it's where we put our timesheets and order forms.

Manager: What do you do to follow up on the out of order parts? **(Clarifying)**

Employee: I don't. I just assume Daisy has it covered.

Manager: This is helpful. Let me see if I've got the process correct... (Manager then restates **(confirm)** *all that was related and thanks the employee for their help. In a later discussion, we will use this example to grow critical thinking skills.)*

Rules and Tools: Consider Options

Request that the employee consider new alternatives to critical behaviors. Encourage the employee to share new ideas, suggestions and anecdotes to help stimulate thinking about new ways to address the issues.

As I shared in active learning tools it is important to help your employees see what options they could choose and how each would affect a successful outcome. The more options they think of the more you have to evaluate with them for best choice.

In that example, here's how the manager might use this as an options lesson:

Manager: Tell me, do you ever have to put the same parts on more than one daily report?

Employee: Sure.

Manager: How long do you estimate it usually takes to get the parts to the floor?

Employee: Sometimes a week or more.

Manager: What seems to be the delay?

Employee: Don't know. Guess it could be the factory.

Manager: Hmmm. They tell me they have a pretty good stock all the time. What else might be happening?

Employee: I haven't thought much about it.

Manager: Let's look at the process you just described to me, what might you suggest if you were running this organization?

Employee: Hey, they don't pay me to run this organization!

Manager (laughing): I know but what if you were in charge, what would you suggest? **(*WAIT* for the response! Important to let them think through this.)**

Employee: Well, I guess I could follow up with Daisy at the start of my shift.

Manager: Good thought, what else? (And it continues.)

The point is to make them think. Keep it friendly and non-judgmental. For some of your staff this may be a very new activity. The more they look at the process the better. Get them to think about their side of the process, Daisy's side and yours!

You can take this conversation even further by asking them to consider what the repercussions are of waiting a week or more for a part. How would clients feel or Sales? What would that do the company's credibility?

Rules and Tools: Apply the information to the real world

> **Consider using a case study or testing the decisions on an actual issue brought forward by the employee to help him/her understand how to put into practice the knowledge they have gained.**

Ask them to give you a scenario. "Tomorrow morning, what will you do differently to create a better work outcome for our department?" or "Next week, when shipping tells you they are running behind on orders, what will you do for or with them or with your clients?"

This is called "Future Pacing" and allows them to paint the picture of behavior that, will be used later in their experiences. They get to "experience" this new behavior in a non-threatening environment (their imagination) and rewrite any negative programming.

Rules and Tools: Closing

Bring closure to the session by:

- **Ask for feedback: ask the employee what new insights they have after this discussion? What will they do differently now and why?**
- **Draw conclusions: When drawing conclusions, give positive feedback on things you saw that you appreciate (insights, suggestions, etc.) Restate your expectations with language that says, "I know you'll do this in the future."**
- **Identify next steps: Make sure to review any open items and give them a deadline to complete or respond back to you.**

Always close the session by *thanking them* for being so open to exploring more effective ways to work. Tell them you plan to support them by noticing every instance where you see them bringing these new behaviors into the workplace. This will let them know you:

- Support them and want them to be more successful.
- Will be observing behaviors.
- Have expectations for their improvement.

Next Steps

After these one-on-one sessions, use a staff meeting to share insights. What did you learn about what you had and had not communicated in the past? How do you view success for the organization? What expectations do you have for the group? Then let them know that you will continue these discussions and use what you learned and what you feel they learned for future performance evaluations.

One last extremely powerful question is to ask the group how they feel you could measure their success. What measurements and methods would offer the most valuable feedback for them and for you? When they help you set success criteria they will have a harder time devaluing it in a performance conversation.

If they are totally unaware of any measurements, this can be a good time to share various reports used by the management team to evaluate the success of the company.

Example
In one organization with a large call center, I was surprised to find the employees knew nothing about the Availability reports[2] or the information on them. When we began to have conversations regarding Time Available, Abandon Rates, etc., the lights went on. Those people who had not been pulling their weight or had spent too much time on Work typing up reports, had no idea that they were causing customer support issues OR that there was a way to measure their productivity. A new expectation was set for the whole organization, as well as a new standard for performance. Those that did not embrace this new standard either opted out of the group or found that the peer pressure within the group was tough to handle. If this is used as an educational exercise and support of staff utilization, and not a hammer for discipline, many organizations find that productivity goes up 10-20% without further conversation.

---

[2] Availability Reports (often called ACD reports) are used to measure how much time the employee stays in the Available mode (ready to take calls,) Work mode (off the call but updating records or other support roles,) and how many customers drop off without being answered. It can also tell you how long the customer waited on line, how long the call took to answer, etc.

In Conclusion

People like to succeed. They like to know how to succeed. They like to be recognized for that success. When they can see how they fit into the success of the organization and can produce a powerful outcome, not only for themselves, but for the group, their participation will grow and the results of the group will increase.

Integration Scenario:

Margaret has taken over a new department. Her first month on the job has her busy trying to sort through the problems in the office. There are customer service complaints and Sales is pushing on her staff for better response time to the customers. Some orders have been canceled because her department is not shipping promptly.

Her manager, Chris calls her to tell her that she really needs to produce some results soon because Corporate Headquarters is talking about out-sourcing her department. Chris doesn't believe this is the answer but needs to be able to report some positive results by the end of the quarter.

Margaret takes a walk around the department and sees some behaviors that cause her to question process and work ethic. She notices some people who are really pushing hard and others who seem to be a little too relaxed.

She reviews all the reports from accounting and shipping. She asks for time on the agenda of the Sales Staff meeting.

Her questions to Sales show her some commun problems as well as who on her staff is a "Go To" person and who the Sales staff avoid when possible.

Margaret plans for her one-on-ones by sending notice to each employee that she would like to pull them off the line for 30 minutes at a time for a brief "introductory" conversation. Then she prepares her list of questions.

Starting with the people she identified as top performers and Sales tagged as "Go To" people, she begins her interviews. Moving through the list of employees, she quickly identifies that top performers have made adjustments for process flaws and understand the impact of their delivery on the company. The others seem never to have had these conversations before and really didn't think there was any impact if they were late getting an order to shipping. Many saw no reason to let Sales know if something was not in stock and definitely didn't think it was their job to rush over and tell anyone that new orders might be delayed.

After these one-on-one sessions Margaret targets the next staff meeting agenda to address what she's learned. Her agenda looks like this:

- What she heard about the current process.
- What she saw as strengths in the organization.
- Best practices that she gained from the employee feedback.
- The goals that need to be achieved by the department and why the company has targeted these goals as important.

- Group discussion on other benefits that they can recognize from these company targets.
- Issues that various people offered as problems in the system.
- Small break out groups on each of these issues. (Two or more people on one issue with the task of brainstorming solutions for process improvements reporting back to larger group.)
- Workgroup selection on larger issues for later meetings.
- Suggestions for future meetings and topics.
- In closing, her expectations for performance of the department and each individual (global expectations) and the metrics she will use to evaluate these.

Margaret determines to set a quarterly challenge for the group. When setting her expectations, she challenges the group to exceed these expectations and allows them to set the prize. (We'll go into more details about this in Rewarding and Acknowledgements- Lesson 5.)

Lessons Learned:

1. What expectations would you most like to address with your current staff?

2. What issues or problems have you identified that could most likely be resolved with this process?

3. What assumptions have you had in the past about staff or process that may keep you from being objective?

4. If you were to ask your employees what success looks like for the department, what do you think their answers would be?

5. How correct are their views?

6. If the CEO were to visit your department or organization and ask what was expected of them, how well would they answer?

7. How well would you answer?

8. What has your manager expressed as his/her expectations of you? What does success look like to your manager?

9. How well could you fully represent successful measurements to the Board of Directors?

10. What part of this process will be easiest for you to do and why?

11. What part of the process will be most difficult and why?

What support will you need to be successful in this process?

Chapter 2

Gaining Buy-In

Change is a constant in our lives. Whether it is voluntary or involuntary, few of us can say that we have not gone through any change in the workplace in the last two years. If you are lucky, it was a smooth transition but most of us have felt the upheaval of change. As I work with clients there are many critical success factors (CSF) for smooth workflow and process change. One of the most important is gaining buy-in. Buy-in is the difference in running and crawling in an organizational setting.

The Basics

While we will have an entire lesson on effortless transitions, here we will focus on the process of gaining buy-in within your group. You won't be surprised to find that communication is a major part of this process. But what and how we communicate makes all the difference in the world.

One of the most important lessons I learned in management was that *telling* doesn't work. In my early years as a manager I was under the illusion that I could *parent* my staff. By parenting, I mean telling them what I wanted and expecting them to do it. Now for those of you that have this type of parent I don't need to give you much explanation of the affect this has on people. For the rest of you allow me an example:

Manager: Tom, you have to start filling in the report this way. You must begin coming in at 7:45 and get the report done and on my desk by 8:00.

Now some of you may be saying, "So, what's wrong with that?" Stop and think about it. Have you ever been in Tom's shoes? Have you ever had someone *tell* you how and when to do something? Is there any part of you that is frustrated or angered by that method? Don't we all want a little flexibility in how we do things? This is when employees start using the term micromanager.

The Intention

There is a careful balance of telling and asking. There are times when telling is appropriate. When the situation is critical or life threatening, there is no time to ask how you would like to leave the burning building. When someone is likely to lose their job by not doing something, be direct. But when their life or livelihood is not threatened pursue the practice of gaining buy-in…ASK them how they can meet the expectations and measurements. Even better, ask them how they can *exceed* the requirements! You'll get better results every time.

Structure and Process

In this chapter we will focus gaining buy-in on a day-to-day basis. The basic steps are to help people see how they fit in to the big equation and then asking them how they can make it even better. You define the "what" and they define the "how." When you allow this process to occur you will find that 90% of your staff will embrace the new process and self-correct.

When we go back to the earlier example, consider how Tom would feel if this was the discussion instead:
Manager: "Tom, this report is vital to the operating plan we establish each day. I need to have it first thing every morning and the following information is important for a complete report...
What can you do to make sure that I have all the data in time for the operations meeting?"

Giving Tom the opportunity to choose when he fills out the report and the appropriate method of gathering the data allows him some measure of control. Don't hesitate to ask, "What else," if you feel you are not getting everything you need. Asking with respect and the intention that Tom wants to do a good job is an important factor in getting buy-in and good results. Put yourself in Tom's shoes and allow him to show you what he can do.

So with the basic rule of "Ask, Don't Tell," let's get started.

37

Pre-session Planning

Where do you feel that there is resistance in your organization? Where would you like to gain more buy-in (translated: more productivity and excellence in your organization?)

If you are going through massive change, reorganization, downsizing or restructuring, how much do your people know or understand about this process and expectations of management?

Consider these carefully to set the stage for your next moves.

After identifying these key elements, ask yourself how clear *you* are on the overall goals of the organization and if you can clearly articulate your expectations. Plan the facilitated session with either your entire group or smaller groups. Ask yourself, "What does success look like?" Be specific in your answer.

Set the meeting announcement with a brief statement as to your intention. Let them know why you are calling them together. Examples could be:
- Make plans with them for how to implement change in the best way.
- Look for ways to improve our process.
- Plan new ways to work with other departments, etc.

Session Opening

Set the tone for the process up front. Let them know that this is to be interactive and you are looking for their input. While you will set the successful outcome, you know your staff will make it work; they are the experts at getting the job done, so "how do we want to make it happen?"

Notice: Put yourself in their shoes. How would you feel if your manager gave you the opportunity to build the process to fit your experience? Feels good, doesn't it? And if you answered, "My boss already does that." Then go thank them for supporting you in such a meaningful way. It doesn't happen in most organizations.

Explain the process of working together

Let them know that this will be an iterative process, that you will continue to meet with them to continuously learn and improve the process. Set clear expectations of the goals. If you want to increase sales by 20% (either revenue or volume,) say it. Be specific about your expectations; so are sales to increase by 20% in revenue or volume? Let them know where they are today and why this increase is important to the company. If it's handling more calls per hour, improving through-put or delivery, tell them the numbers and the company goal. Then spend some time talking about why this is important. What does the company hope to achieve with this increase?

Now let them know how you want to move through the session. We'll be using a powerful group of questions that help facilitate the brainstorming.

Rules and Tools: Use active learning tools

Experiential activities, such as opportunities to practice applying concepts, interaction with manager on specific topics, hands-on demonstrations, role plays, etc. all stimulate the employee to participate actively, rather than listening passively to the conversation.

The key is to get them involved. When you see opportunities to get them up and out of their chairs during the discussion, take it!

Example: Bob, the manager, lets everyone know that the company wants to speed up the manufacturing line to deliver 20% faster. Bob's group is responsible for delivering the parts to the line. Due to the limited space around the line, you cannot have too many parts on the floor at any given time. Up to now, that has not been a problem because of the timing currently in place. Now with the mandate to process 20% faster, you'll need to develop new processes. Depending on the size of the group, you can break them into smaller teams to discuss parts of the process, like warehousing and then have them report out to the larger group. Or you can keep the group together and facilitate the session.

Note: It is very helpful to talk with your coach or a consultant on various ways to facilitate these sessions. If you don't have one available, talk with a trusted advisor or your HR or training coordinator. Since they have to

facilitate so many activities, they can help you see good options.

Note: You may also find that it will support the group (now or later) to have someone from each side of your operation to work in this session. For instance, someone from the Warehouse and someone from Manufacturing to support the thought process or once you have developed the plan; invite them to the next meeting to review and comment on your suggestions. You'll find this invaluable for increasing buy-in.

Focus the discussion

- At the top of a flipchart, write in bold letters the goal: *speed up delivery of parts delivery by 20%*
- Next, ask the group what they already do well? *In other words, where do they already deliver fast and effectively?*
- Be sure as they make comments that you ask them what makes that work? *Do you do anything special to make that work so well? What specifically do you do to make that work? (Using the word specifically makes them look deeper into their activity.) You are looking for either motivators or skills OR just plain genius!*
- Now look deeper into the process for differentials. *What else might they suggest that you could do more of, better or differently?*
- Look for excitement. Ask someone to come up and draw the floor layout or chart the process. *When there appears to be enthusiasm (even humor) capitalize on*

it. Ask for deeper participation and let it be lead by individuals in the group.

- When people offer a statement or suggestion, comment positively and write it down on the flipchart. Even if it's a small idea. No criticism or limits here. We're brainstorming!
- Once you have a broad range of options, ask them to look through them and consider which ones would make the most impact. What would bring the most benefit? Which ones need more definition or consideration?
- Then ask for people to experiment with the ones they feel are best. Ask them to try it for a few days or a week and then report back to the others on what they found.

Consider Options

If they get stuck or seem to be thinking too hard, *take away gravity*. What do I mean by that? Take away the current situation, broaden it, narrow it – make it different in some way that opens their eyes to new possibilities. *Example: Suppose we had more room? Or suppose there was a higher ceiling, lower floor, more money, less money... anything* to expand the options.

One powerful way to get them thinking is to offer a story about a time when you were stuck with the impossible and came up with an idea that everyone thought was silly. Then share how you tried it anyway and with minor tweaks, you made it work and improved the situation. If you don't have a story of your own *borrow one*! People learn a tremendous amount from metaphors (stories.) That's why I share examples as we go along. Those case studies help you look at others and then evaluate how it applies to you in a very non-threatening way. We'll look at this in the coaching module.

Consider using a case study or testing the decisions on an actual issue brought forward them understand how to put into practice the ideas they have proposed. In a later module on process development, we'll look at this further but for now, consider asking them to "walk through" the current process and determine where they get bogged down. Before they get lost in issues and complaints, say to them, "As you walk through our current process, think of the places that slow you down. What would you like to do to speed it up, move it out of the way or change it to make you more efficient?"

I always like to throw in the thought, "You know this might actually be fun. What if we could get so efficient that we started having a *good time* in our work?" Then I paste a silly grin on my face and say, *"No, we wouldn't want to do that, would we?"* It takes them off guard and can get them to laugh. When they laugh they add oxygen to their brains and we're off to a whole new start!

Ask them to give you a scenario. "Tomorrow morning, what would you like to do differently to speed up the process?" Again, this is future pacing and is a powerful anchor for new behavior and thought process.

What to do if they get emotional?

If for some reason someone gets upset or overly negative, reassure them. They are only acting out of fear. The new goal may appear threatening to them (in some economic times that can happen easily.) Reassure them that you are asking for their help because they are the experts at getting the job done and you want them to be part of the process.

If they can not engage, there are times when it is best to call a short break and then talk with them quietly, allowing them to go back to work if they just don't want to participate. I have never had to go this far because the process is so engaging, but allow yourself the permission to make this call if you need to do so. Just be sure that you do this privately and graciously. If you create another "Negative Nellie" (more about her in the Enhancing Perception,) you'll have more problems to deal with than you care to have.

Closing

Hold to a time limit for this session. Have a clock handy and call time on your facilitation 10 minutes before the end. You may have only gotten started when you hit your time limit.

Let people know that you respect their time and that this discussion will continue at the next meeting. In the meantime, you want them to keep looking at the process and come back with even more ideas. For those that have volunteered to experiment, remind them of their commitment and tell them you look forward to their insights.

Rules and Tools: Closing

Bring closure to the session by:
- **<u>Ask for feedback</u>: ask the employee what new insights they have after this discussion? What will they do differently now and why?**
- **<u>Draw conclusions</u>: When drawing conclusions, give positive feedback on things you saw that you appreciate (insights, suggestions, etc.) Restate your expectations with language that says, "I know you'll do this in the future."**
- **<u>Identify next steps</u>: Make sure to review any open items and give them a deadline to complete or respond back to you.**

Always close the session by *thanking them* for being so open to exploring more effective ways to work with their team and you. Tell them you are looking forward to their continuous improvement efforts. If you plan to bring in others from various departments, remind them of that procedure.

In Conclusion

By asking for your employees support and assistance, you will naturally create buy-in. Don't be surprised by two things.
1) They may be slow to respond if you or other managers have never asked for their opinion before!
2) The excitement once they catch on to the idea that you actually value their feedback.

Some managers worry that they will get nonsense from their staff in these sessions. While you will have some people who offer some off-the-wall suggestions, you will find that the group will self-correct. As you go through the list, they will tell you what will and won't work. By having them focus on what will be the most effective and give the "most bang for the buck," they will be supportive of only those ideas that will succeed. I have always been successful, no matter how "poor" the team, when I have offered them respect and encouragement to succeed. People always pleasantly surprise me with their hidden potential.

A story to consider:

The traffic was backed up for miles and the police and road workers stood on the side of the busy highway scratching their heads. A huge trailer truck was stuck under the overpass. It was several inches too high and had now become lodged beneath the bridge. Many people stood outside their cars waiting for the road to clear. A young boy and his mother stood together near the workmen.

"What's wrong, Mommy. Why aren't we going to Grandma's?" the small boy asked, cuddling his teddy bear.

"I'm sorry, honey. We'll go soon but you see that big truck over there? It's gotten stuck under the bridge and the policemen are trying to get it out." The mother responded.

The boy studied the situation carefully and then said, "Why don't they just let the air out of the tires?"

The policeman nearest the little boy stopped his conversation and stared. He threw back his head and laughed. "Out of the mouths of babes! Never underestimate anyone, boys! Let's go get that truck loose!"

So as you see, anyone, any where, can have the answer you're looking for if you just listen.

Ask the right questions in the right way and you'll get there even faster!

Integration Scenario:

Jim was being asked to reduce breakage on the server line. While it was a small number of units damaged each quarter, the cost of each server was enormous. Management wanted it to be zero and was not very tolerant of excuses.

Jim had a good group for the most part and he didn't want to beat them up for a few misses. However, radical process changes needed to be considered. Management wanted his plan in one week. While Jim walked the line every day, he could see little that his people were doing wrong.

He called his group together and presented them with the new goal.

Jim: "Folks, I'd like to spend sometime on our quality and safety issues. As you know we occasionally have accidents on the line. I'm always concerned for your safety and I'd like to make sure that we are as profitable as possible. If you consider that a server costs the company $100,000 per unit, when one falls off the line, it's an ouch heard around the world." (smiling)

Jim: "I'd like your input on what we can do to improve our process. The target I'm looking at is 100% delivery every time. What are your first thoughts on this goal?"

The feedback Jim receives is mixed. Some people are ready to come up with ideas, a few are defensive.

Defensive employee: "It's not our fault when they fall off the line. We didn't do anything wrong."

Jim: "I appreciate how you feel and I want to be clear that this meeting is not about placing blame. I want all of us to explore together as many ways as possible that we can increase our delivery. You all are the experts. You know where the line works for you and where the process works against you. I'm open to all suggestions. All those that we can implement quickly, we will. I'll advocate for all the rest. Agreed?" (Jim looks at *each* employee for agreement.)

Jim: "Now what do you think we do best on the line? What are you proud of?"

The feedback begins and Jim writes these on the board. As each suggestion comes to him, he checks with the group to see if all are in agreement. If not, he asks the person to expand on that thought. As the process moves along, there are many ah-ha's. Jim captures them all. When the ideas slow down, Jim asks the next question.

Jim: "Now what would you like to do more of, better or differently?"

Suggestions from the floor are numerous and Jim moves to a second flipchart to capture their ideas.

After they slow down, Jim steps back from the chart and says, "Wow, good work. Which of these could we do today without any hesitation?"

As they call out their choices, Jim circles them with a different color marker. After they finish, he asks if there is anything else they would like to add. One or two have additional suggestions. Jim marks these down and asks, "Can we do them right now?" When they nod yes, he circles them also.

Jim: "Now, let's look at your suggestions and consider which ones will have the most impact. These should be our absolute must-do items."

Several of the items circled now get a star and a few that have not been circled are starred as well.

Jim: "What do we need to do these that are starred but not circled?"

Some feel that they need permission and others feel that the equipment needs to be altered. Finally, one hand in the back slowly rises.

Jim: "Mark, do you have a question or suggestion for us?"

Mark: "Well, I'm one of the people at the end of the line where this usually happens, unfortunately. It's nothing deliberate but I do have problems with the cart that the server slides on to."

Jim: "What problems do you have?"

Mark: "Well, there are latches that are supposed to close around the server as it slides back onto the cart. However, some times if the server slides on crooked or not far enough back, it doesn't latch. When we start to roll it away, WHAM, it falls. The server is so tall that there's no way to catch it."

Jim: "That must be pretty scary and upsetting."

Mark: "Even more so, now that I know what it costs!"

Jim (smiling): "Yeah, it's a big hit to the wallet, isn't it? Mark, what would you suggest?"

Mark: "I'm not sure but there ought to be a way to know that it's secure."

John: "We also ought to have a way to make sure that the cart is lined up perfectly and that the server is coming off straight."

Sally: "Is there a way to build better side supports so that when the server tips something will catch it?"

The group engages readily now and everyone becomes very focused on the process of getting the server safely off the line.

While some retooling for the cart and some minor process changes become necessary, Jim has successfully engaged his people in the commitment to the company's goals and thoroughly bought in to the process. Jim will continue to follow up with the group and will plan rewards and acknowledgements (a later lesson) for their participation and suggestions.

Lessons Learned:

1. Where would you like to have more buy-in with your group?

2. What areas of your organization or process would you like to improve?

3. Where do you believe you may find resistance?

4. What did you learn in this lesson that will help you overcome this resistance?

5. What specific actions will you take to address these areas of improvement?

6. Do the actions require your entire group or smaller sub-sets?

7. What outcomes do you hope to achieve with this process?

8. If your facilitated sessions come up with ideas outside of your outcome, how open to these new ideas are you?

9. How clear is your staff as to your expectations?

10. Will this process be a surprise to them? If, yes, then what actions did you see in this process that will help you guide them comfortably into it?

11. How open will your supervisor be to the recommended changes offered by the group?

12. What might be necessary to prepare your supervisor for the recommendations, before and after the sessions?

13. What else do you feel you need to support you before you begin?

14. When do you plan to start?

Terah Stearns

Chapter 3

Building High Performance Teams

We have a lovely lake (part of the Colorado River) that flows through the center of Austin. At various times of the year there are punting teams that practice their rowing skills along the lake. It is always very interesting to see their progress throughout the season. Punting boats are the long narrow boats with 5 or 6 crew members. They use long oars and can speed along the water incredibly fast. When they reach their true power, they seem to fly across the water as though they were motorized.

In the early part of the season though, they aren't quite so efficient or graceful. At times, just watching them get in the boat can be quite amusing. Once they've mastered this small but important feat, they then need to learn to hold the oars, and synchronize their movements. This again is no small occurrence. Because of the length and therefore, weight of the oars, they must build muscles throughout their bodies to support them. At first they are incredibly uncoordinated and then week by week, you see them get stronger and more coordinated.

When the season begins, the oars seem to flap through the water and you hear them clinking against one another. Finally, they have the muscle, the skill, the coordination, and most important, the ability to use the oars and listen to the captain. They now have the basics down well enough to apply part of their attention to the calls being made. Focus becomes a part of their skill set. The captain has learned to observe and command thereby building the team to their highest ability.

After only a few short months, it is exhilarating to watch them fly down the lake. It is precision and confidence in action. It is a joy to watch and from the smiles on the team's faces, I'm sure it is just as much fun to be in the boat. What power and precision! Wouldn't it be wonderful to see your organization moving through their day with such joy and synchronicity?

The Basics

While sports are a great metaphor for any team, there are levels of complexity that help them reach their peak performance. The same is true for your organization. Understanding the key factors and how to polish your team to such precision is powerful. It depends on the nature of your organization and the current capabilities and health of your group how fast you will be able to create such a powerful team. Here we will look at these key factors and determine some tools that will optimize your team.

The Intention

I have yet to work with a group that did not *want* to be a strong team. Some people fall naturally into a team structure, some processes require a strong team and others appear to work very hard to make it happen. I believe we all work happiest and best when we feel supported. My signature line for years has been, *together, we succeed.* I intentionally chose it years ago because I know that I cannot stand alone. The complexities of any organization are too great for one person to do it all.

Besides, one person will soon plateau and if they push beyond that plateau, they will peak quickly and then begin to fall. It is a simple physical dynamic. And frankly, it's no fun!

The intention for building strong teams is to agree that everyone has something to offer the team and that everyone can contribute. Now, I can just hear some of you saying, "But I have people on my team that are not capable, not competent, not..." Lots of these statements are rolling around about individuals on your respective teams. I will grant you that we do not always have all the right players. That would make life *too* easy (and then anyone could do your job and the pay would be very small indeed!)

Our intention is to make your team the best they can be and as they pick up momentum, you will find that peer pressure will help the others pick up the pace or self-select out of the organization. It will also be easier to set "powerhouse" expectations and know that they will be supported by the larger group.

Structure and Process

So many factors go into a great team but for the purposes of this chapter I will share some basics and how to work with them. All of these work hand-in-hand with other parts of the book, like setting expectations and gaining buy-in, and the more you study them the better you will be at creating incredibly effective teams. You'll see with each technique or tool you implement your team will respond better and better.

Now, what goes into a great team?
1. the right people
2. the right skills
3. the right attitude
4. mutual goals and expectations
5. commitment
6. empowerment
7. buy-in for the outcome
8. a recognition and acceptance of their differences
9. methods for successfully dealing with issues
10. Rewards and recognition for a job well done
11. and last but not least, LEADERSHIP at all levels

Wow! Great list, huh? Just for grins, take a moment and determine how high your group rates on each of these. Use a scale from 1-5 (5 being highest (excellent) and 1 being lowest (non-existent.)) Then find the average of your grade points. Obviously, 50 would say you are reading this to just refine and maintain your team leadership. Anything less than 30 and we need to pay close attention to all the lessons in this text, not just this one!

In the next sections, I am going to give you some fun exercises to get your group to move into *awareness* of teaming. You may also want to consider some coaching to go beyond these steps and by pulling together all you will learn from these lessons you will become a more powerful leader..

First, we'll look at various personality types and how they can work together more effectively. Then we'll look at a teaming exercise that will create awareness of the power of a team In later lessons, we'll address how they can communicate more effectively and address issues easily to prevent dysfunctional behavior.

Pre-session Planning

The first step is to consider your staff. How well are they currently working together? Do some of them work very well together and others seem ostracized? What is the tension level in the group? Who are the peacemakers and who are the instigators?

While we will not spend too much time on the instigators (later chapters on coaching, performance and communication will address these,) it is important to understand who will be the people most resistant to teaming.

I'm asking you to focus on what's working. Where are the groups or individuals who will be the most positive support and provide essential and constructive peer pressure? These will become your positive change agents.

The first step will be to set expectations (where have you heard that before? *Chapter One, right?*) What's important to you about shifting your group through these exercises: efficiency, better handoffs, less stress, less in-fighting, more support for process or organization? You name the reasons, outcomes or benefits. Always begin with the end in mind so you'll know success when it appears!

The second step is to share awareness of personality types and how they interact. Make this a fun exercise and share it in a way that has no judgment. We are who we are. If we understand what makes the other fellow tick, we can meet them half-way more easily and create positive exchanges that build great relationships.

The next step is to take them through the Group to Team exercise listed later in this lesson. Study the instructions carefully. This exercise is developed to have them come to the recognition on their own that the team is more powerful than the individual or the group. And, YES, there is a huge difference in Group vs. Team. We have a tendency to organize people into groups and assume they will become a team. It happens only when there is natural leadership in the group and willingness to reach a mutual goal or a large enough crisis to make people put aside their differences.

The last step is to bring it all together and continue the awareness on a regular basis. Rewarding behavior that shows great teamwork and coaching behavior that misses the mark is a key to maintaining a healthy organization. There are two chapters on rewarding and coaching.

Remember, if you lose your focus or forget what you have worked hard to build, your staff will see it as just the management agenda item of the day and your credibility will be diminished.

Session Opening

Set the tone for the process by setting the expectation. Put this in the most positive terms you can so that they will stay open and participative through the process. It may be that this conversation with your staff is coming about after having a series of one-on-ones with them. Or it may be that you have done a "mini-physical" on the organization (explained in "Enhancing Perception") and find that you'd like to counteract some negative perceptions draining the group's energy.

A powerful opening might be, "We've been working together for a while and I thought it might be fun for us to explore some ways that help us work even better together. Each of you have specific strengths and competencies that add to the whole group but we've gone through a lot of change over the last year(s) and sometimes that redirects our attention away from our strengths. Would you agree that could be the case?" PAUSE here and look to each individual for a head nod, murmured agreement or some sign that they are engaged. "Thank you, I'm going to ask everyone to participate and share in the process."

Next question, "Given that we all agree that we've had a lot of changes and that we would like to work better together, tell me what *working better together* would look like?"

Capture the responses on a flipchart. Go around the table and ask for each person's response (we want EVERYONE to participate!)

Next question, "What would be the benefit if we could achieve this?"

Capture the benefits and go around the table again, maybe backwards this time (to keep them engaged and on their toes.) When you ask for each person's response, you are saying that you value each of them and their opinions AND expect everyone to participate. This is everyone's issue and outcome!

Exercise #1

Using a brief introduction, like:
"Because I work with each of you from a little different view, I get to see the unique characteristics of each individual and the blend of these characteristics in the group. I think it's helpful to see how these relate so I've developed a couple of exercises just to help us learn more about each other and how we may need to be communicating more effectively."

Show this chart and ask them to quickly decide which symbol identifies them best. Have them write their choice down on a 3x5 card and turn it over.

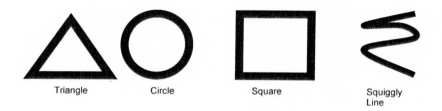

Triangle   Circle   Square   Squiggly
                                                   Line

Now, hopefully, you are hearing some laughter and some funny comments, if not, don't worry. This isn't a deadly serious process. We want them to engage and understand.

The next step is to ask them to just raise their hands for a count of how many are a:

    1. Triangle   4
    2. Circle   3
    3. Square   6
    4. Squiggly Line   1

I've taken the liberty of putting numbers beside these so that I can explain the rest of the process.

Now smile at the group so they know you are having fun with them. Turn to the chart and ponder it (with the smile.) Even add a, "Hmmm," if you'd like. Have fun with it.

"So let's see what you just committed to," (smile again.)

"Now before I begin, I'm going to be giving you some generalizations around these forms. The fact is that each of you has *some or all* of these characteristics in certain situations but for the sake of our conversation today, we'll pretend you are *most like* the one you chose." Feel free to make this fit your conversational style but make sure you get this point across: in each of us, we have ALL of the symbols. We each have a more dominant characteristic and one might be almost invisible but we all have each. At various times in our life we can shift from one to another as we adapt to our environment.

Our Triangles are the drivers in the organizations, they may only see the big picture and don't necessarily care for lots of details. They want to see forward momentum on a pretty consistent basis and may not be the ones to chat around the water cooler. They want results, consistently and no questions.

Our Circles are the people oriented folks. They really like to socialize and want everyone to be happy and work together. They like details and like to be sure that there is consensus on every decision. They would make great party planners!

Our Squares are very detail oriented and prefer to have all the facts before making a decision. They are not necessarily people oriented and like working alone with the process clearly defined.

Now the last... "Have you ever been in a meeting and everyone seems to be coming to agreement and all of a sudden there is this voice...from the back of the room...that says, "wait, we haven't considered this or this, OR what if..." and you all groan and sit back down. (MAKE SURE YOU SMILE THROUGH THIS!) That's our squiggly line. They are very creative thinkers. They can't imagine the life of a Square. They are out there...thinking of new possibilities more than seeing how it all fits together. They are not always very detail oriented.

Hopefully, you are hearing some real laughter here and people are looking around to see *who the squiggly line is.* You'll know who they are because they will be hiding or laughing and nodding.

Now, smile and say, "Thank heaven we have some of all of these types. It gives our organization even more capability. If we were all the same, we'd be impossible to work with and we'd quickly plateau."

"Sometimes those differences create some issues because we expect everyone to want and need the same things we do. If we are a square, we feel everyone needs the details and should be giving us as much detail about issues as we would like. However, that same need for details drives the triangle nuts! They are driven toward the big picture and find details mildly to aggressively annoying (depending on how much of a triangle they are!) Squiggly lines on the other hand like to investigate all the possibilities and keep drawing new pictures. Imagine what that does to the square and triangle!

"The good news is that none of this is bad. It's helpful and supportive. There is a wonderful balance of energies and abilities when the group has some of each."

Other Commentary

What's important to realize is this very mix gets the job done. If you only had triangles, you'd find that there would be too many painting the big picture and driving for results but no one doing the actual work or not checking for quality! If you had all circles, they would spend so much time making sure that everyone was happy you'd never get your work done.

If you had only squares you'd spend a great deal of time addressing the details, process and procedures and there would be no drive for results. If you had only squiggly lines...you'd never even get to a project! You'd continually be coming up with new ideas and never have any work done!

These are gross exaggerations for best understanding of the types. There are even better tools for these personality profiles such as Myers-Briggs® or the DiSC© (which we use in our facilitated sessions with clients) but this simple tool gets the message across and allows you to get the team thinking about the differences.

What you want them to understand is that all of these types are good and useful. We also tend to look at everyone else as being *just like us*. A Square cannot imagine why a Triangle doesn't want all the details. The Triangle can't understand why the Circle wants everyone to agree! And almost all of them can't understand why the Squiggly Line is so *out there all the time!*

Rules and Tools: Use active learning tools

> **Experiential activities, such as opportunities to practice applying concepts, interaction with manager on specific topics, hands-on demonstrations, role plays, etc. all stimulate the employee to participate actively, rather than listening passively to the conversation.**

Consider playing some scenarios with them. These help them realize the various personality types and their needs. It helps them take off their screening mechanism and step into another type's awareness.

You can make the following questions into a game or just have your staff explain their reasoning. It is in the process of exploring this reasoning that they begin to understand.

You could also have the various types explain why they wouldn't choose to have and why.

- What kind of car would each type buy? Why would they choose that kind of car?
- If you were giving a presentation to (choose a type) what kind of presentation would you give them? How much detail? How long or short? Here's where some coaching will really come in handy! *Example: if a square were giving a presentation to a triangle –what would work and what wouldn't? Why?*

- What type of profile do they think you fit? What makes them think you are that type? Be sure to take this lightly. Laugh or chuckle as they tell you what they think you are and why. Let them know that their awareness is a good measure for you. It helps you understand how they are viewing your behavior and knowing what profile *they are* will help each of you communicate better.

- One of my favorite exercises is the following. Read the question but don't give the answer. Let them come up with it.

  o Four types are going to take the elevator. The first type steps on the elevator as soon as the door opens and presses the button for the floor they want. Who might that be? (Answer: Triangle!)

  o The second person gets on just as the door closes and sees someone else coming down the hall and holds the door. What type is that? (Answer: Circle.)

  o How is the Triangle feeling? (Answer: annoyed, anxious to get a move on!)

  o Now just as the third gets on, a fourth squeezes in. One of them is the square. What might the square be looking for as they enter the elevator? (Answer: Some fun statements come up here. They might be looking to see if the elevator has been certified and met inspection. They will definitely check the date on the inspection sticker! They might check the weight limits for the elevator and quickly calculate the total weight of everyone to be sure we are in compliance! You get the picture.)

o Now the fourth person is what type? What might the squiggly line be doing on the elevator? (Answer: Just about anything, from commenting on the décor and what would make it more pleasing, to your outfit, tie or improvements to the building. They are the creative types and may talk your arm off making suggestions, sharing ideas, showing you their latest drawings, necklace... They are a ball of energy and will be totally into their own world and drag you along with them!)

o You can then add to this by asking them to tell you what each might be wearing on this elevator. This gets fun as well and helps them integrate the lesson.

Second exercise

As you go through the personality exercise focus on individuals and when necessary talk about group rather than team. You'll see why this is important in a moment. For the sake of time, you can do these two exercises in separate sessions. Not everyone can afford to have their staff away from the job for more than an hour. Personality types take a good 30 minutes to an hour if done correctly. You don't want to limit the discussion too much because that's where the awareness begins.

For this exercise, you will need about 15 – 20 minutes. If you can allow more, great!

On a large flipchart (a couple of pages behind the first, so the letters can't be seen through the paper) make a triangle of 25 letters like this:

R
S V I
W P Q O B
N C X Z M A T
L D S K U W Q Y F

Now skip two pages on the flipchart and make another triangle of 25 letters like this:

Z
B R Q
T X E N P
N D M C R A L
K Y O W V I J S U

Here are the steps. Follow them carefully for maximum results:

- Tell them that you are going to give them a *memory test* just for fun! (Listen for the groaning and laugh with them!)
- Ask them to get out a pencil and paper (if they don't already have them in front of them!)
- Tell them: *In a moment I'm going to show you a chart of letters. I will give you 10 seconds to look at these letters. Memorizing as many as you can in the order they are given. I will then cover them back up and you will have a moment to write them down to the best of your ability. Are you ready?* Don't repeat the instructions. That's part

of the awareness. At most, just say, memorize as many as you can.

- Now look around the room and notice anyone holding their pen. Laugh and say, pencils down... this is a memorization test not a *"how fast can I write test!"* *SMILE when you say this!*
- *Get ready to turn to the first letter triangle but don't show it until you are ready to keep time.*
- Now have your stop watch ready or your second hand on your watch available. If you don't have either, just say in your mind, 1001, 1002, 1003...1010...*Stop.*
- Give them exactly 10 seconds and then cover the triangle and tell them to write down as much as they remember.
- As soon as they are finished writing, tell them to grade their own test. Uncover the first triangle and remind them that the letters must be in the right placement to be counted. For example: *original chart*

R
S V I
W P Q O B
N C X Z M A T
L D S K U W Q Y F

- If they wrote down,

R
VSI

- They would only get 2 correct. Even though they remembered all the letters, they only got two in the right place. This usually annoys them, but just smile and say, "that's part of the fun. Besides, I'm not grading you…too much!"

• Now on a separate flipchart (you'll want this to be visible later on,) make three columns but only put a heading on the first column. Put "Ind."

• The flipchart will look like this:

IND		

• Now go around the room getting each individual's correct score. You may have some that get only 1 and one or two that will get as many as 12. I have seen some that get as much as 16 but the group usually demands a recount. That's fine, don't worry.

• Now the chart will look like this:

IND		
1 3 4 2 7 1 **3** 3 9 4 5 1 3 2 1		

- Now take a rough average of the individual scores and write it on the chart. (Like the 3 on the chart above.

Focus the discussion

- Now pause for a moment and ask them what they *experienced in this exercise.* You are looking for them to say just about anything from frustration, anxiety, lack of direction (Squares!) or fun. Make some notes around the numbers. You don't have to go around the room to each person just capture a few comments.
- Now break them into groups of 3 or 4 (depending on the size of the group.) Try to divide them as equally as possible (2 would be too small a group.)
- Ask them to look at their results again (still having the triangle of letters viewable) and combine the results. For example: if the person who had the

73

R
VSI
Were grouped with someone who got
SVI
And someone who had
R
TGI
W P Q O B
Then their total merged score would be:
R
SVI
WPQOB

2

- You'll find the energy level in the group will go up dramatically and there will be lots of laughter. When they look like they have their answers compiled, go back to the chart and add the second column.

The chart will look like this:

IND		Group	
1		12 **13**	
3		15	
4		13	
2		11	
7		9	
1	**3**	capture their comments here	
3			
9			
4			
5			
1			
3			
2			
1			

- Now ask them, "What do you notice now?" We are looking for them to say that the scores are better. Then ask, "What does that say about the difference between group and individual performance?" Obviously, they'll talk about the power of group for improved results. They might also say it allows other people's strengths to support the effort (especially those with high scores combining with those of low scores!) *Still do not mention team, even if they do. Just write down their comments!*
- Now hide the first triangle of letters and say, "Now staying in your groups, I'm going to do the same type of memorization exercise. I'll give you some time to prepare. We are looking for the same outcomes as the

previous exercise. So take 30 seconds to prepare."
*Notice that you still gave them very little instructions.
It's fun to watch them. Do they immediately start
strategizing together? Some of them may ask for
permission to talk among themselves. Say, "Yes, hurry!"
I use this time to find the second chart and get ready to
turn it open but it also allows them to form a plan. If
they are paying any attention at all!*

- Now open the flipchart to the second set of letters and
  begin the countdown. Only give them 10 seconds as
  before and then cover the chart . Tell them to write their
  answers and quickly correlate their letters. When they
  appear to be done, show them the chart again for
  scoring.
- On the last column capture their scores. You should see
  much higher scores and even perfect scores of 25! You
  should also see some happy faces. *Don't write TEAM in
  the third column YET!*
- Now begins the really important discussion. Here are the
  questions to ask:
    o What did you notice about this part of the
      exercise?
    o What was different for you this time around?
    o What was more powerful for you?
    o What would you do differently if we did this
      exercise a second time with your group?
    o What do you think this exercise is all about?
- The first time someone says the word *TEAM,* <u>pause</u> and
  say, YES! TEAM! And write it on the top of the column.
- You may not have to ask all the questions. What we are
  looking for in this exercise is the awareness that while
  we are better in a group than individual, we are

POWERFUL in a TEAM! But what makes the difference between TEAM and Group? It's up to them to discover the difference and express it through the exercise. *Remember: If you tell them they won't remember. Ask them and it's theirs for life!*

Consideration

All too often we are reorganized into a group and <u>expected</u> to operate as a TEAM. (NOTE: this is an important thing to say to your organization, especially if it is true for your department or business.) Then management wonders why they do not get the performance level expected.

You want to make sure that the discussion goes beyond the exercise. Keep these flipcharts and bring them to future meetings to continue the discussion. If you can continue while they are still "in the moment" then here is where to take them next.

- Given that we have seen that team is more powerful and *fun*, what can we do to operate more effectively as a team?
- What would that mean in terms of behavior?
- What could we do to keep that sense of fun and accomplishment in our organization?
- What else?
- How do the personality types figure into this?
- How are they useful?
- What else did you learn today that will make this an even better place to work?
- What else did you learn today that will make *your* job more fun?

77

Let them get fired up about this and then ask them to be prepared in subsequent meetings to revisit even more ideas. Challenge the current "memorization teams" to come back to the next meeting with ideas for improvement. Tell them you'll have a "prize" for the group with the best or most ideas. *(We'll discuss ideas for prizes and rewards in a future lesson.)*

Then make sure you follow through. If this is just a fun exercise and falls off your radar, it will fall off theirs and you will lose credibility.

When times are tough, you'll be able to use this new awareness to outperform everyone else in your business unit!

Rules and Tools: Closing

Bring closure to the session by:
- **Asking for feedback (what did they like best? What was most useful?)**
- **Drawing conclusions**
- **Identifying next steps (what will they do when they leave the room today? Future pace them!)**
- **Or simply sharing information about the experience of the session.**

Always close the session by *thanking them* for being so open to exploring more effective ways to work with their team and you. Tell them you plan to support them by noticing every instance where you see them bringing these new behaviors into the workplace. This will let them know you:

- Support them and want them to be more successful.
- Will be observing behaviors.
- Have expectations for their improvement.

In Conclusion

When these teambuilding exercises are used with focus on growing awareness and critical thinking they become a powerful adjunct to the many other lessons in this manual. You are helping your team understand your expectations. You are making them a part of the solution and you are setting the stage for managing change and supporting one another in the future.

When you are through with the exercises, take time to review what *you have learned.* Review the *Lessons Learned* questions in the Integration Scenario and ask your coach for further support in taking this to a whole new level. This is not a one time occurrence. It is a building block for your future success!

Integration Scenario:

Jennifer was asked to create a new quality assurance group. While the company had always talked about quality there had never been any one department to focus on results. She had many challenges to overcome with this new endeavor. Not everyone was going to appreciate having someone test their work and most were unaware of how far Jennifer hoped to go with this new option for the company. She envisioned not only a test group but also a group to oversee and document quality throughout the company, maybe even going for a quality certification or award some day. For now, she had to create the right group and make it into a powerhouse team that would be respected by the whole company.

Jennifer was not able to hire all the right people. Some people were assigned to her because they were tired of programming all day and wanted to do something different. Others were considered "cast offs." As one manager put it, "They either get this right or they're out of here!"

With a sigh, Jennifer set her sights on building her team. She knew that with any new organization, setting expectations and building a vision were her first priorities. She would spend time with each individual to get to know them and then begin the process of helping them integrate into a true team.

After several sessions around mission and vision, she saw some momentum. Her meetings on expectations seemed to excite many and she felt it was time to begin the team strategy sessions. She prepared the conference room with her flipcharts from previous sessions to remind the group of the organizational goals and expectations. She brought in bagels and juice and set up her two flipcharts ahead of time. On the left hand flipchart, she turned to the third page and carefully drew her four symbols. About 3 pages beyond that she drew her first letter triangle. Then turning two more pages, she laid in her second triangle of letters.

As her group filed in she greeted each one with a smile and welcome, asking about fishing trips, family and the latest news on their various projects. Inviting them to grab some food and drink, she made them feel like part of *her team.* Promptly on time, she asked them to have a seat and to get started.

"Good morning and thank you for getting here so promptly this morning. As we've gone through some of our sessions, you know that being timely is one of my expectations and you are living up to them beautifully. I appreciate that.
"Since we've spent so much time on setting the vision and expectations, I thought it might be good to have some fun today. Now, I know that fun is not something we are supposed to have at work but if you won't tell, I won't!

"To get started with this I'd like to show you a little chart. When I uncover the chart I'd like for you to pick your favorite symbol and just write it down on the card in front of you. You can draw it or just write the name of it on the card."

She uncovers the chart with Square, Triangle, etc., and then begins the discussion as above. She takes them through the exercises and then calls a 15 minute break.

When they return, she has moved the symbols over to the wall with masking tape for future reference.

"Now that we understand *who we are,*" she says smiling, "let's look at how well we work. No pressure there, right?"

"I'd like to give you a little memorization test." Groaning and complaining ensue.

She smiles and says, "This will only hurt for a few seconds." And then she proceeds to work through the rest of the exercise.

As they finish with the questions, Jennifer begins to feel a higher level of camaraderie in the group. The group decides it would be fun to put their *symbols* on the walls outside their cubicles to remind each other of how best to communicate with them. The Squiggly Line has another idea and the whole group teases her about "too many ideas and to stick with the plan." This is a big win for the group as the Squiggly Line tended to be an outcast or the group tended to let their aggravation show.

As Jennifer thanked them for participating she asked them to keep their groups (from the memorization exercise) intact and come up with more ideas for encouraging Team. She has a nice little prize for the winner in the next meeting. Tom smiles and says, "No problem, we've got *Squiggly* on our team!" Everyone laughs and cat calls of "no fair, that's cheating!" echo around the conference room.

Jennifer is given lots of congratulations and thanks as they file out the room. While she is tired, she's learned a lot and loves the excitement as she sees the "team" come together.

She just might have the Quality Department fully vested *sooner* rather than later.

Lessons Learned:

1. What new awareness do you have after reviewing this lesson?

2. What do you see now in relation to personalities that you may not have been fully cognizant of before?

3. What profile type do you think your supervisor is?

4. How will you interface with him/her differently now?

5. Think of your team. How many Triangles do you think you have? How many squares? Circles? Squiggly Lines?

6. When giving directions or communicating expectations, what will you need to do differently for each of the personality types?

7. In what areas do you realize that miscommunication or even lack of communication could have been happening due to these various types?

8. In what areas of stress within your organization might these various types be contributing to? In what way? How might you resolve this?

9. What behaviors will indicate to you that your group is now a team?

10. What outcomes do you hope to achieve with these exercises?

11. How will you deliver these exercises? In one session, in multiple sessions, in an off-site?

Chapter 4

Coaching

Coaching is a powerful skill for any leader. When you are an *effective* coach, people learn faster, engage more completely and support change rapidly. A great coach creates a *safety zone* for people to explore alternatives and make better decisions. You stimulate a learning environment that raises the energy and adaptability in your organization. This takes practice and support but when you become highly skilled at coaching, life is fun and engaging at all levels.

The Basics

One of the most important lessons I had as a young manager was not in the workplace. It was an opportunity to observe a gentleman coaching a little league baseball team. He was a terrific coach and made everyone feel like a winner. One day I asked to take him to lunch. I had watched him work with young children and seen the incredible patience he had. I knew he had been handed the team so it wasn't a recruiting success. He was known for winning more games than any other coach in our town. I wanted to know how he did it and see what I could incorporate into other areas of my life.

Our lunch was terrific and Jim was very generous in his comments. Here are some of the keys I review frequently:

1. Everyone is good at something. A coach looks for *talent* and then puts it in the *right position* to benefit the whole group.
2. A coach sees more potential in you than you know and will push you beyond your limits to be even better than you thought you were capable.
3. While the coach knows you can do more, he gives you training drills to slowly build your muscles and test your abilities.
4. Small successes consistently recognized will help people move mountains, one rock at a time.
5. It's the coach's job to see which rocks to move first and to keep everyone focused on their part of the plan.
6. The coach sets the boundaries for the team and helps them realize their responsibilities.
7. The coach calls the shots and lets the poor performers go when their heart is not in the game. It's the coach's job to make the hard calls. When the whole team is being diminished by the one, it's time to make the call.
8. While discipline and honesty is a big part of the coach's job, the team has to feel good about what they are doing and see it as fun and rewarding.

Each of these was so powerful and beneath each rule were even more powerful lessons. It seemed so simple until I began to uncover the real meaning behind each one.

Contemplation on each of these is worth the time. Let's look at how they work together in a business setting.

The Intention

Knowing <u>when</u> to coach is as important as knowing <u>how</u> to coach. In most organizations you will see two different types of managers. There are many types but these are the two extremes. One is very directive. The other is the parent. Neither is effective all the time. There is actually a sequence to each of these behaviors and places where they are more effective than others. You do not want to get stuck in parenting mode. It can be exhausting and is not really acceptable in business. However, the concept of nurturing new skills is powerful so I will use that definition for now.

Your job as coach is to:
1. Review your people to decide where and how they can be most effective.
2. Guide them with discipline and honesty.
3. Support their success and give them an opportunity to celebrate.

Structure and Process

So when do you coach? Whenever you need someone to step up to more effective behavior is a short definition. You can also use coaching to help someone who is struggling with a career choice or just to see a new way of doing something.

A coach is part cheerleader as well as the one who charts the course. Throughout these lessons you are seeing one coaching technique after another. From setting expectations (critical for planning and disciplinary actions) to performance appraisals and performance improvement plans. All of these require coaching skills and will greatly benefit your outcomes if you keep the right intention and focus.

The steps to coaching are:
1. Determine the one topic that is most important to address.
2. Feel comfortable articulating what you'd like to see and why you think this might help them or the organization.
3. ASK more questions than you talk.
4. Assure the learning and development happens on their side; not yours! (Although you cannot help but learn something in the process.)
   As Jim put it, "the work is theirs, the success is theirs. I can't run the laps for them nor can I hit the ball for them. It's their job to gain the skills to a level that they *win* more than they lose!" Now that's a coach!
5. Listen for what stops them and then ASK some more leading questions to help them define what THEY can do to fix it or make it work.

Obviously questions are the way to go, so what questions do you ask and how do you ask them? Let's look at the basics.

Planning

Throughout these lessons, you'll notice that we ask a great deal of thought provoking questions. That's to help you learn and integrate the material. I just set the context, you make it fit and develop your own style. I once knew a terrific sales person who wanted to become a coach. He wanted to teach people how to be better sales people. Now, I wanted to have this skill because frankly, as a small business owner, I no longer had a large sales force out there creating deals for me.

What I saw in his style though showed me that while he was a great sales person, he didn't know how to coach. *He just wanted me to do it his way.* He had a set of questions, scripts and processes that he used very effectively: *for him*! He felt by teaching me these and grilling me on them, I, too, would be successful.

Have you ever had this experience? Have you ever had someone intent on making you do it their way? What was the outcome? How successful were you at being them? Take a moment and consider this.

What we tend to do is try to fit people into our mold and expect them to be successful because that mold was successful for us! Good intention but how often does it work? In the chapter on Building Teams we saw clearly that there are different styles and ways of thinking. One size does *NOT fit all!*

89

How many people in your life have used this method on you? How successful was it? Did you become even more resistant to what was being suggested?

Many people tell me they become very resistant. Most tell me that the method of telling and forcing the script was their parents' method and their teachers' methods.

Now what would make us become so resistant to something so well intentioned? Before you turn the page, please think about this. Just give it a second...There is HUGE learning here.

The Process

The most powerful process in coaching is to ask someone what they would most like to see as a positive outcome. What would they like to accomplish?

Then ask "what would that look like if you were doing it today? Or had it today?"

Next confirm what you heard. Try to use as many of their words as possible to be sure you *both* heard the same thing. Look at words that are vague, like "I'd do a *better* job." What does better specifically mean? Be sure that you ask them to clarify in a friendly, supportive way or they'll get defensive and you'll go nowhere.

Author's Observations: Coaching is a very fine art. It is 60% intention and 40% communication. The intention is that they want to get better and *you believe they can be!* Of the remaining 40%, communication is made up of effective listening 60%, 20% feedback/clarification and 20% provocative, effective questions.

Now ask them what might be some of the benefits to having accomplished this?

And *always* ask "What else?"

"What else?" is an incredibly powerful question when asked with positive intention and supportive tones.

My clients tell me I ask them until they become uncomfortable but the truth is that when they become slightly uncomfortable it's because they are really hitting the truth. People tend to hide the truth in phrases that they think others want to hear. We don't like to open up and be *really honest.* They think, "You may not like me if I tell you my real truth." The truth is that we like people better when they are honest and even vulnerable.

A master coach creates such a safe environment that people learn that it is *fun* to really go down deep and hit the truth then bring it up and *go for it!* It is peeling the onion. You have to get rid of the dry outer layer and then peel away many layers before you get to the rich, juicy flavorful part. That's where the real magic happens! It's amazing how much we have covered up over the years, wearing all the masks that people have assigned to us; most of which don't fit or never did.

Explain the process of working together

The next step is to set some goals. What are some activities that can be done to show positive movement toward

91

success? At first, it's best to set baby steps. Gaining small successes and having them report on them as they gain mastery over their new skills.

The one good thing I got from the Sales Coach was that I needed to call people after an engagement to get feedback. Now he set this in the context of cold/warm calls. Since I hated cold calls my resistance went up enormously. But when I realized that people might have more questions or might even (now get this!) want me for future engagements or other support AND that they were genuinely excited by my speeches and trainings, well… What can I say? I call after all my engagements now or send e-mails of thanks. The rewards are great.

What's important to realize here is that as my coach, he could have done several things better:
- He needed to spend more time getting to know me.
  a. What was important to me?
  b. What was threatening to me?
  c. Then we would have moved faster and more successfully.

Most people just want to TELL you what *they do* and expect you to go do it the same way. This seldom, if ever, works. What you will find is they will go out and try it your way and then go back to their own style *OR worse*, throw out your idea as stupid or not acceptable and not respect your support in the future. Either way, you lose momentum. As a coach, one important thing to do is make sure you are doing "ecology checks." Always ask, "What fits for you in this situation?" or "How would that work for you?" Then offer, "What could you adapt to make it more your style?"

If you are creating the right environment with powerful, effective questions, you will find they are developing their own style anyway.

Rules and Tools: Use active learning tools

> One of the most effective ways to get people to learn or adapt behavior is to do an end-run. Tell a story. People learn a tremendous amount from metaphors (stories.)

I share examples as we go along to help you evaluate the process and determine how it would work for you. The case studies help you evaluate how it applies to you in a very *non-threatening* way. After all, it's my story, right? You can take it or leave it but most of the time because your mind stays open for the punch-line or purpose of the story; you hear it in a more resourceful state. You get to rent it and test drive before you buy!

When people feel defensive they are NOT resourceful. As a matter of fact, they are spending more brain power trying *not* to let you in. They are pulling apart your suggestion so they seldom really hear any of it – much less the punch line.

So tell a story. Even if it's not your story to begin with, feel free to copy it, add to it, and revise it to fit the situation. Rent some of mine until you find your own. It's okay, you're coaching. The more important outcome is to help the other person achieve their desired result.

Think about where I have shared stories with you here. As I told the stories, did you hear possible dialogue for you? Did you build pictures in your mind of what it might have looked like for me to have lunch with the little league coach? Did you wonder whether he was old or young? Did he look like your old coach? What feelings came up for you in the sales story? Could you feel my anxiety or resistance to his methods? Could you see yourself in a past experience? Ninety-nine per cent of the population will live the story with you...*in their own way*! Let them. That's the point. They are in a highly resourceful state in those moments.

The key is to tell the story and then ask an incredibly powerful question.

For instance, I'll repeat part of the sales story for you and you can watch for the question.

What I saw in his style showed me that while he was a great sales person, he didn't know how *to coach. He just wanted me to* do it his way. *He had a set of questions, scripts and processes that he used very effectively:* for him*! He felt by teaching me these and grilling me on them, I, too, would be successful.*

What would you recommend to him to make him a more effective coach?

Now go back to the original paragraph, earlier in the lesson and look at the questions I asked you there. All of them are geared to make you think more deeply and relate it to your own life.

The power of story is to share it without pontificating, have a purpose (a point) and bring it to a *solid conclusion*. I didn't do that here because I was developing your questioning skills but when I tell the story in live training I usually have people with very strong reactions. Why? Because at some point in of our lives, most of us have tried to do sales. From vacuum cleaners to encyclopedias, from magazines to telemarketing, many of us have tried to supplement our income by selling something. A majority of us would rather have a root canal without anesthetic than have to sell anything ever again!

So another rule is to try and find something with which your employee can relate! If you are telling a story about neurosurgery and your employee has never even been to the doctor, you're in trouble from the start.

It is also powerful to use experiential activities, such as opportunities to practice applied concepts. You may use interaction on specific topics, hands-on demonstrations, role plays, etc. all to stimulate the employee to participate actively, rather than listening passively to a conversation.

For instance, if they are having a problem communicating effectively with certain team members, allow them to role-play a conversation with you as the other person. Or do role-reversal where they have to BE the other person and you play them. This is a great way to allow them to see how their style might conflict with others and better yet, they will have to consider what the other person may be seeing, hearing or feeling.

Then go back and ask some effective questions around what they noticed about the way they felt or the way they think the other person might have felt. Again, ASK, don't tell!

Rules and Tools:

> **Adult learning research shows that adults prefer to learn by validating information based on experiences rather than simply accept concepts at face value. It takes more preparation to have a session with good experiential learning exercises, but if you are interested in having employees develop a deep understanding of the business or subject, it is worth the effort.**

Focus the discussion

- One VERY important point is to pick one topic per session. Don't try to peel all the layers of the onion in one meeting. You'll both be totally drained and too exhausted to work. You may also have them feeling very bad about themselves if you try to *fix* them all in one day.
- Remember small successes lead to enormous success! *You can move the mountain – <u>one rock at a time</u>!*

Rules and Tools: Apply the information to the real world

> Consider using a case study or testing the decisions on an actual issue brought forward by the employee to help

him/her understand how to put into practice the knowledge they have gained.

Ask them to give you a scenario. "Tomorrow morning, what will you do differently to work more effectively with your team?"

Ask them to tell you of a time when they handled a similar situation better. What did they do differently? What do they notice were keys to that success? What would they have added to the successful scenario that would have given them an even better outcome?

Rules and Tools: Consider Options

Request that the employee consider new alternatives to critical behaviors. Encourage the employee to share new ideas, suggestions and anecdotes to help stimulate thinking about new ways to address the issues.

What to do if they get emotional?

The best thing to do is not get emotional in return. Emotions are usually just an indication that you are getting close to the real issues or truth. If they cry, pass the Kleenex and keep talking. Or you can say, "I'm going to get us some water. I'll be right back." Step out of the room, get the water and resume the conversation without comment. When they try to apologize, say, "don't worry about it. We all have things that really affect us from time to time. That one just caught you by surprise."

97

If they get angry, you get quiet. Remain reasonable and the less said the better.

I once had a guy screaming at me that nothing was his fault. I sat back and breathed. It took a great deal of concentration just to breathe so being quiet was easy. When he finally got quiet, I still sat quietly. After a moment or so, he got very uncomfortable. He then asked, "Aren't you going to talk to me?"

I paused for a moment and then said, "I'd like to talk with you but you seemed to need to vent for a while. If you're ready we can continue. The important thing for both of us to remember is that this is to help you. I found it hard to help when you were yelling at me. (Pause here.) I do know that sometimes it is uncomfortable to talk about change. (Again, pause.) If you'd like to work through this, it's important to me that you become more successful. What would you like to do? "

He wasn't necessarily happy with my response. From observing him with others, I knew this was his way of getting others angry and I wouldn't take the bait. If I responded in kind then he would feel justified. That wasn't what I was there to do. After another minute of silence, he became more uncomfortable and then apologized and said he was ready to talk. So guess what our discussion was about?

There may even be times when you realize that someone needs counseling (psychological counseling) rather than coaching. Don't hesitate to refer them to your company's employee assistance program or HR for support. It's not your job to diagnose only to manage the process and lead people to excellence.

Rules and Tools: Closing

Consider how the employee can synthesize the information session.

Bring closure to the session by:
- **asking for feedback,**
- **drawing conclusions,**
- **identifying next steps, (in coaching there should always be follow-up steps and report outs in succeeding sessions. The season doesn't end with one game!)**
- **or simply sharing information about the experience of the session.**

Always close the session by *thanking them* for being so open to exploring more effective ways to work with their team and you. Tell them you plan to support them by noticing every instance where you see them bringing these new behaviors into the workplace. This will let them know you:
- **Support them and want them to be more successful.**
- **Will be observing behaviors.**
- **Have expectations for their improvement.**

In Conclusion

Coaching is about believing that people are capable of more than they are showing you. It's about asking them what they want and then helping them determine how *they* can get there. It is a co-creative process and should be considered an honor to develop staff beyond their current patterns. Ask, tell good stories and believe in your people.

Integration Scenario:

Phil is meeting with Rob who is a good employee but has a tendency to get very angry and act out in unproductive ways. He has never threatened anyone but people really feel uncomfortable with his anger.

After asking him to consider new behaviors, sharing a story or two from Phil's past and asking very effective questions, Phil tests Rob's awareness. While Phil knows he has the concepts, he is still not convinced that Rob has integrated the coaching.

Phil asks him to think of a time in the past when Rob would have gotten very angry but either did not become upset or controlled his anger very well. Once he saw from Rob's facial express that he had something in mind, he asked him to tell the story. Phil listened carefully as Rob spoke. He listened for the words and tones he used. He looked at posture and what triggers kept him from going off the deep end?

Rob shared that he was recently working with his young son on the car. He couldn't get a part to go back in correctly and got very frustrated. He was about to lose his temper when he saw his young son's face looking intently at his work. Rob stopped what he was doing and realized that he didn't want to cuss in front of his son or throw anything. He didn't want to scare his son.

Instantly, it became clear that he had a gentle loving side toward his son. It was not that he had uncontrollable anger; obviously he could control it. He gets very angry when he becomes frustrated. Phil decided that Rob must care deeply about doing a good job and making things work.

(These are very powerful moments both in coaching and as a leader. Recognizing the good side of your employees and that there is a way to help them.)

Now, using questions, Phil guides Rob back through the story.

Mgr: Rob, I noticed that you seemed very focused on getting the part in, was that the case?

Rob: Yeah, I had probably been bent over that hood for a good hour.

Mgr: That's pretty tiring, isn't it?

Rob: Yeah. I can remember my back being pretty stiff the next day.

Mgr: Now you mentioned that you felt the tension building. How did you know you were about to get angry?

Rob: Gosh, I guess I never thought about it before.

Mgr: Well, just for a minute, step back into that situation. Feel yourself tense and frustrated. What do you notice?

Rob: Well, my stomach is knotted up and my back is hurting. I feel my throat getting tight and my fingers are really not working well. I'm really getting mad at them because I'm fumbling with this stupid part so much.

Mgr: Rob, I want you to take a deep breath right now. Would you believe I can *see you* getting angry! (Phil smiles.)

Rob: Wow, you're right! I was actually getting mad all over again.

Mgr: What's important to notice is that you can create it at will and let go of it at will. After I asked you to stop and take a deep breath, what happened?

Rob: Well, it took a couple of seconds but I could step out of it.

Mgr: Yes, you did and you're right. You can step out of it any time you choose. That's a pretty powerful feeling, isn't it?

Rob: I guess I never thought of it that way before. But, yeah, I guess I can.

Mgr: You did it easily when you saw your son's face, didn't you?

Rob: Yeah, he looked so cute. He was staring so intently at the engine parts. It was like he was mentally trying to make it go in.

Mgr (laughing): I'm sure you wished he could have.

Rob: That would have been very nice at that point.

Mgr: So what stopped you?

Rob: He was so intent that I knew if I let out a roar I'd scare him to death. I really don't want him to ever be scared of me.

Mgr: Rob, that's the nicest thing I think a parent could ever say. What if I told you that sometimes you scare your co-workers?

Rob: (Totally confused.) What do you mean? I'd never want to do that. How could I?

Mgr: That reaction says it all. I felt you might be unaware of this. Sometimes when you lose your temper on the line, your co-workers don't know how far you'll go. You can get pretty angry, you know?

Rob: Man, I never meant to scare anyone. Really! Man, no wonder some of them aren't very open with me.

Mgr: Rob, the important thing is to notice here that you don't <u>intend</u> to scare anyone and that you <u>can</u> control your temper. Especially when you know that others might be uncomfortable.

Rob: Absolutely. I never meant to make anyone uncomfortable.

Mgr: I think that's a given. So let's explore some ways for you to handle your frustration. What I notice is that part of it comes from the fact that you are so dedicated. That's a quality we don't want to lose, right?

Rob: Yeah, I guess. (He's still considering what his actions meant to others.)

Mgr: Rob, I don't want you to beat yourself up about this. You can always let others know that you didn't mean to be so angry. You could ask for their help or you could just buy them a beer after work and let them know you're sorry. What we want to do now is set some new behaviors that will prevent the anger, right?

Rob: Yeah, sure.

Mgr: The good news is that you are aware of how the anger feels when it's building. We know you can stop it if you notice it. And that it's not acceptable to you that you scare people. Are you in agreement on all of this?

Rob: Yes.

Mgr: Now, what could you do in the future that would help you notice and prevent the frustration?

Rob: Well, I could stop and breathe every now and then, like you had me do a while ago.

Mgr: That's a good start. Breathing is always a good thing around machinery.

Rob: I could also...

As you can see there is a lot of give and take here. You want to keep clarifying that they are picking up the same points. You want to be sure that they don't lose focus on what they do well. All you want to do is ADD new positive behaviors. Read through this again and look at what else *you* might want to do in this situation. What else might have helped Rob?

Lessons Learned:

1. What's the idea behind the safety zone?

2. What were the main points from the little league coach?

3. Which did you like best and why?

4. Considering the people you work with what are the top three things you would like to start coaching them about?

5. How would you lead into these three topics?

6. Look back through the lesson and determine which questions you like best and make a list to work with in the future?

7. What other questions could you create to support your coaching?

8. Given the three items you most want to coach your team around, what stories would support these?

9. When you have chosen the stories, write them down and then edit them to the shortest and most succinct points.

10. What questions could drive home the point at the end of each story?

11. Try the stories out on other people (not your employees) and ask them what they liked best? What was unnecessary? Did they feel the power question was strong enough to make the point?

Terah Stearns

Chapter 5

Enhancing Perception

One of the most interesting characteristics of a group is the power of perception. I have watched groups of people move from solid performers to "negative Nellies" in the space of 90 days. It all starts with a negative perception of one or more team members. In the book "Getting to the Heart of Change" the authors, Doug Krug and Ed Oakley, comment on the DNA principle. It's quite simple and I'm sure you have seen the process work in many ways at many times. Someone makes a Decision (D) which can be good or bad about another person or organization. The issue becomes critical when the decision is negative. Once the decision is made they will only Notice (N) the activities or characteristics that support that decision. I have always coached people that it is like putting on blue sunglasses. All of a sudden, all you see is blue! From there, they begin to Acknowledge (A) to themselves and others *their observations.*

In a healthy group, you will see other team members share the opposite view to counter the negative impression. However, what frequently happens is people will pause, go back into their memories and recall a similar response or incident. Now who among us has *never* had a bad moment? I'm quite sure you could choose anything about anyone and be able to support that response and create an immediate negative perception.

This bears critical attention and understanding so that you can help stop it in its infancy and help others understand what's happening.

The Basics

I enjoyed the concept of DNA when I heard it because I have worked with so many organizations over the years where this was the real issue. When negative perceptions are prevalent in a group, the energy level is depressing at best. The amazing thing is that we do this to ourselves! Trying to tell someone they are wearing "blue sunglasses" is a terrific challenge. If you *only see blue* <u>the rest of the world is wearing the wrong color glasses!</u> People will get very mad when you try to raise their glasses even a little bit off their nose. After all, they've been operating on an assumption *they made* and now you are telling them they are wrong!

Shifting this is a mix of psychology, coaching and support.

The Intention

It is important for the manager to understand that people really buy into their perceptions. Once in place it is not easy to change them. If you try to *tell* them they are wrong, they will only grow angry. You must be supportive while leading them to new conclusions. The only way to change a perception is for *them to see it differently.* Patience is a virtue here. When I coach managers and teams, we can have a breakthrough in an hour or a year. It really depends on how long the perceptions have been in place and how safe the group feels. If they feel threatened you will find they will dig in their heels even more and fight to maintain their position.

Structure and Process

The first step is to recognize when negative perceptions are taking place in your organization. Surprisingly, many managers don't or won't see this until they have massive problems. It is not effective to go "looking" for negativity (you will always find some,) however, you also need to be open to your people and the temperature of the organization.

It is helpful to have a baseline. A colleague of mine, Laurel Barton (www.oswegoconsulting.com), dubbed it the "organizational physical." Just like going to the doctor for a physical, you should have some specific questions that you ask on a relatively frequent basis. The frequency will depend on the size and complexity of the organization.

Let's say you decide to set the baseline and "check-up" on a quarterly basis. The system is very easy and can be very rewarding. First because your people will feel heard and second, because you will know the "temperature" of the group.

Make it a point to sit down informally with each direct report. By direct report, I am focusing on the people you directly manage. After visiting with the direct reports, if you feel further analysis needs to be done, select a random number of *their* direct reports and ask similar appropriate questions. (This is assuming you have managers reporting to you.) Remember, your intention is to support the well-being of the staff. You want to catch the negative perceptions early enough to make the change easily before they become too wide spread or too ingrained in the organization.

What you will notice in the process is whether people are operating openly and with confidence or not.

It is important to recognize that emotions come in two varieties, resourceful and unresourceful. When this becomes second nature you will be in a better situation to deal with the issues of the people around you. Resourceful emotions – such as love, acceptance and confidence – clarify and strengthen someone's ability to see things as they are. While unresourceful emotions – such as anger and fear – feed upon themselves, distorting reality, making a difficult situation even worse. Obviously, emotions are a powerful factor in determining how someone will act or what they will do or say. The wrong emotion, experienced at the wrong time, can seriously jeopardize relationships or projects.

These resources or lack thereof, create levels of tension.

When you feel fully supported:
- you are more confident;
- you will take more risks;
- there is less tension.

When you feel that resources are limited: money, time, people, or tools:
- you are more tense;
- you have less confidence
- You take no risks.

Now review your people. Evaluate their level of tension and perception of their current resources. You can see how these factors can increase the level of tension and the smallest things can set off a chain reaction.

As tension rises, people can become more physically, intellectually and emotionally active, but their relative productivity is a very different matter. As tension rises productivity falls immediately and dramatically. This is a stress reaction I'm sure you have seen many times. In a climate of layoffs and downsizing, this stress reaction can create a very unhealthy and even anorexic organization. Learning to address this effectively and supporting people through their issues is key to keeping the business healthy and productive.

Pre-check-up Planning

Before starting, consider how *you* feel the group is working. Look for the following:

- Do you hear pleasant hall conversations? *In organizations that are becoming negative, you will see a significant lack of camaraderie. You will notice some stealth activities, such as private whispering and looking over their shoulders as they converse. While this may be planning a surprise birthday party, it often means trouble for the organization.*

- Do you hear spontaneous laughter periodically? *Even in the busiest work environment there should be some expression of good humor; even self-deprecating humor is very healthy and healing.*

- Do you see people volunteering to support each other in meetings and at their desks? *When staff truly values each other they will naturally solicit and volunteer help.*

- How often do you hear positive, supportive suggestions for business improvement and individual performance? *In very secure, positive environments, you will see people pushing the envelope to be the best and counseling each other to be better and more efficient.*

While these are just a few of the thoughts to set your course they can be invaluable in testing the health of your group. The last question to ask yourself is "How often do I smile and laugh?" If you do not answer "frequently...daily...hourly;" check your level of negativity! The power of perception may be working against you also. It's best to find a coach or internal support system to help you reset your perceptions before you try to address your staff's issues. If you are feeling downtrodden and then try to listen to others who are down, you'll all drown.

The Check-up Sessions

In the chapter on managing group dynamics and staff issues there are some key aspects to creating effective one-on-one sessions with staff. However, it is more effective to do the "check-up" in an informal manner. If you don't normally have quick "cubicle conversations" with staff or have staff that are hard to interrupt (like a call center) then you may want to use the techniques described for one-on-ones.

Plan your questions with the thought that they may happen over several quick cubicle conversations or have two primary questions that you can ask in the hallway or break-room to make it appear impromptu.

Types of questions to consider

While I'm sure you will come up with great questions on your own, I find it helpful to have some standard questions to build upon. Consider any of the following:
- What would you say are our biggest strengths?
- What would make us even more efficient?
- If you were to give our group a grade from A to F, what would you give us? What criteria did you use for that grade?
- If you could change anything in our group, what would you change?

- What do we do best?
- How well do you feel our team works together? What would help make it better?
- What would you like to see me do to support you better?

Use active learning tools

It is important to notice where negativity starts. When people have been very caustic about someone or something, it is powerful to ask one of the following:

- What do you think made them choose that course of action?
- Could there be something else at work in that instance?
- What positive intention might they have had for doing that?

What you are attempting to do is to get them to look at the other side of their current perception. Consider this carefully. What other questions could you ask to help shift this view?

Focus the discussion

Be sure that as you visit with people you are keeping focused and holding a strong intention to improve the relationships. If your group is very negative, you will need to work harder at keeping this intention. It can really get you down so do it in small increments and work with your coach or support system to detoxify your system occasionally. Remember, this is not about you. It's the way they made the original decision. We want to find when and where and why they put those blue sunglasses on so that we can make it easier to remove them.

One of the best ways to manage this is to remember that they are all basically good people. They've gotten lost in their decisions. We'll help them turn back on the lights and see new options.

Consider Options

As you ask your questions and evaluate where people are stuck, it's good to ask them what they might do if they HAD to change that perception.

Example: Charlie has a very strong, negative feeling about Christa. He feels she does not pull her load or deliver on time. As his manager begins to review the issues, he asks Charlie what he has experienced that created this perception. Charlie begins a litany of instances that show Christa is not doing her job well. What is interesting about the list is that most of them have not been experienced directly by Charlie. Only one instance was an issue with delivery to Charlie and Christa was only 3 hours late for major project plan details.

Mgr: Charlie, I noticed that most of these issues are things you have heard from others and not directly impacting you. How did you learn about them?

Charlie: Mason told me.

Mgr: Were each of them directly related to work Mason is doing?

117

Charlie: I don't know. He just seemed really mad at Christa.

Mgr: So Christa has only been late by 3 hours for that one project plan?

Charlie: Yeah.

Mgr: Was she late with this before or after your conversation with Mason?

Charlie: It was after, I think.

Mgr: How many projects is Christa working on?

Charlie: I don't know.

Mgr: Is she working on more than yours?

Charlie: Yes. I know she's working with Mason and Tom.

Mgr: She pulls all the data from the various developers, doesn't she?

Charlie: (A bit more thoughtful.) Yes, she does.

Mgr: Do you think they give her data their top priority?

Charlie: (Grinning sheepishly.) Probably not. They don't even give me much priority.

Mgr: Hmm. What do you feel she does well?

Charlie: Well, most of the time her data is really well done. She doesn't just pull data; she extrapolates good outcomes and plans from it. She is always cheerful and I don't have to do anything to the reports she turns in. She always seems to have a good grasp on how Tom's and Mason's projects will impact mine and that's really helpful.

Mgr: What else do you like about her?

Charlie: (continues)

When we uncover that perception is not the full reality, we frequently set the tone for the options phase to be very effective. Before you begin to invite these options be sure that there is not a real performance issue at risk. Be sure that there they are beginning to realize their issue is purely perception (even someone else's perception!) This takes diplomacy, timing and power communication skills (more in a future lesson on this.)

Apply the information to the real world

When someone is really stuck in their perception consider using a story to reveal where you have gotten caught in bad perception. The story should support the idea that we all have situations where the impressions of others have created difficulties for us. If you do not have a personal story you would feel comfortable sharing, it is fine to use a story about someone you know or that they respect (as long as it has good effect and a positive outcome.)

What to do if they get emotional?

Remember in this situation that they may be operating under the fear of being wrong. You are challenging their decisions and they are less resourceful than normal. Keep this understanding and don't push too hard. When you notice they are beginning to become tense and less responsive slip into story mode to make it more about someone else rather than their decision process.

If the tension begins to increase, find a graceful way to end the conversation and pick it up again on another day. The majority of people shift easily when they realize this perception is harmful or does not serve them. It is most important that you do not *force the fix*. They must shift on their own through your coaching and support.

In Conclusion

All of us have had times when we have made decisions about individuals that have proved later to be false. Realizing that it takes vigilance and commitment to constantly evaluate our decisions takes a strong character. When an organization supports this with positive peer pressure and effective questioning, coaching and mentoring, it becomes more powerful and a great place to work.

The energy drain on an organization of negative perception is enormous. People close down and become increasingly unproductive when they feel under pressure from others. Consider a time when you felt that you could do nothing right, how effective were you? How many risks would you take? How hard would you push to make things happen?

Helping the individuals in your organization remove their colored sunglasses and see value in each other starts with you. Keep your eye out for the positive implications of a healthy organization. Reward your people for *positive* peer pressure and make it an ongoing value within your organization to support one another, to look for the good and not the bad. You'll enjoy your management position and they'll be excited to be part of such a great team.

Integration Scenario:

Cameron had been managing his group of developers for over two years. The pressure on the new software project was creating some turmoil with tight deadlines and lack of resources. Everyone was working overtime and the tension in the group was growing stronger. He used to hear good natured jokes across the cubes, now he occasionally heard cursing and angry exchanges. Knowing that stress can make even the best people unresourceful, he began an "organizational physical." He chose the following questions:

- *What do we do best?*
- *How well do you feel our team works together?*
- *What would help make it better?*
- *What would you like to see me do to support you better?*

He asked these in random order according to the mood or length of discussion.

When asking about team work, he found that there were two people that were "not pulling their weight." He also found that the team felt that he was not communicating with them enough and this was creating some additional antagonism. He realized that his lack of communication was out of respect for their workload but they saw this as not caring about them. He let them know that he would make a better effort and still respect their busy schedules.

Once he found that two people were targeted, he first began to evaluate their work. Both appeared to be doing a good job although one spent more time at breaks than others. The other programmer left earlier than the rest. Before making any judgments, Cameron watched more carefully. He found that most negativity from staff was directed at these two and primarily at the young programmer, Tom, who left early.

Cameron observed that Tom was at work before he came in each morning. He stopped by one morning to say "hello" and asked how long Tom had been at work.

"Since 5:00, sir." Tom said.

"Wow, why so early?" Cameron asked.

"Two reasons. One, it's quiet and I get a heck of a lot of work done. Two, because I have to leave early to pick up my daughter at pre-school. I don't want to leave the team without doing my part. The deadlines are too crazy."

"Is this new with your daughter? I don't recall you needing to leave early before." Cameron asked.

"Yeah, my wife has had to get a job and it's pushing us both. She takes her to pre-school before work and then I pick her up. It's bad timing with this crazy schedule here at work. I worry that the guys are feeling I'm letting them down." Tom said.

"Have you told anyone about what you're doing? How you are handling the work load?" Cameron asked.

"Naw, I didn't want to whine. It's my problem, not theirs."

"I understand but I think it might help the team. We're all pretty close and when people start spending their energy worrying about why someone's not here...well, you know what I mean, don't you?" Cameron smiled and lifted his eyebrow.

"Yeah, I guess I do. I've felt some tension from the group on several occasions."

Cameron laughed, "Yeah, they aren't good at hiding their feelings, are they? How can you let them know what's going on without making a big deal out of it?"

Tom smiling, "I'll probably tell Kerry. He's got the biggest mouth and...heart. Then I can also send some e-mails when I first get in. Jackie always notices the time stamp on things. She never fails to mention when someone's working late. She'll particularly mention 5:00 a.m. because she is NOT a morning person!"

"No, that she is not. That's a good plan and I'll support you where I can. By the way, let me know if you need anything. I can't always do everything I'd like to for you guys but I'll always do my best. Okay?" Cameron shared with a grin.

"I've always felt that was true. Thanks for waking me up to the group's perception."

Now as Cameron began to review the other programmer, Janice, he observed the breaks were longer than acceptable. He coached Janice on the breaks and perception. She shared that when she got stuck on a problem, she would go outside and walk around. She would go over the code in her head and then go back to make the changes necessary. Then she'd test it. She could see how this would create a negative perception and offered to modify her breaks.

Cameron waited for this shift in behavior to change the group dynamics. When it didn't he carefully worked with people to see that Janice had changed. This was a very diplomatic discussion. Without sharing that Janice had been coached or reprimanded, he worked to have people see the value of her code.

Cameron started with Matt who had been with the company the longest and held the most negative view of Janice.

Cameron: "Matt, I noticed you seemed a little annoyed with Janice at the meeting. Anything going on?"

Matt: "Yeah, she really bugs me. I told you about her last month, remember?"

Cameron: "Yes, you said she took really long breaks, right?"

Matt: "Yeah, really long breaks."

Cameron: "I've been observing her for a while now. It seems like she's taking fewer and shorter breaks now. Have you noticed?"

Matt: "No, I just noticed she's never at her desk."

Cameron: "Does she do her work?"

Matt (grudgingly): "Yeah, just too many breaks."

Cameron: "What does she do on her breaks? Do you know?"

Matt: "No, she's never shared."

Cameron: "I wonder…do you think she could be working on programming problems? I know when I was programming I always liked to leave the code for a while and clear my head."

Matt: "Could be but it doesn't look good."

Cameron: "Matt, do me a favor. We have such a tight group; it's difficult for any of us to be upset with the other.

125

I'd like for you to consider or even ask Janice what she does on these breaks. Do you think you could do it without upsetting her?"

Matt: "I don't know. I don't think it's my place to ask."

Cameron: "True, it wouldn't be your place to reprimand her. But it might be good for both of you to have a conversation about the breaks. Just to understand what's going on; not to change it. What do you think?"

Matt: "I don't think that would be a good thing."

Cameron: "I can understand your hesitation. I might feel the same way in your place. I just keep thinking about a time a few years back when someone was really upset with me. I was keeping some pretty late nights working on a project and I'd come in late the next day. Some nights I'd be at work until 2:00 or 3:00 in the morning. So when I came in late, I felt justified.

"The problem was I wasn't sharing any of this with others. They knew I stayed after they left but not how late. What was difficult was they just got mad rather than asking me what I was doing or why I was late. Of course, I learned from that and began sharing with my co-workers what I was doing. It didn't prevent me from having a really bad two months with fellow programmers. The tension was really bad.

"Maybe Janice could benefit from knowing why you are frustrated. What do you think?"

Matt: "I guess I could try. I've been in the same situation you were in and it wasn't fun."

Cameron: "Tell you what. You talk with Janice. If you don't feel better about what she does then let me know. This team is too important to me to see it fall apart. We have one of the best teams in this company, don't you think?"

Matt: "Sure, I wouldn't want to work in any other department."

Cameron: "Then I really need your help. None of us have the energy to waste on being frustrated with each other. We're too good for that."

Matt: "Agreed. I'll try."

Later that same day, Janice poked her head in his office. "Thanks for talking with Matt. He came out on one of my breaks and talked with me. When he found out what I was doing he offered some great shortcuts to finding some of my errors. I may not need as many breaks in the future!"

Lessons Learned:

1. What did DNA stand for?

2. What makes this a powerful concept?

3. How could it help you in managing and coaching your staff?

4. In doing a quick "physical" on your organization, where might there be issues or concerns?

5. In recognizing these specific issues, how might you use the techniques in this lesson to resolve "or heal" the organization?

6. How might you share the concept of "blue sunglasses" with your staff in a fun and enlightening way?

7. What sort of preparation or support will you consider before approaching staff?

8. How might this shift your staff to more productive behavior?

9. What other benefits might you see from using these techniques?

10. How often should you take a "temperature check?"

Terah Stearns

Chapter 6

Planning and Growing Leadership

At an early stage in my career, a mentor suggested that I would never be promoted if I did not create a successor. It was powerful advice. You can not move forward if management does not feel that there is someone to replace you effectively. The last thing a company wants is to create a hole in the organization. Growing new leaders creates more opportunity for you and even if the promotion is not imminent, your job will get easier with more people to support you effectively. Leaders do that with ease.

The Basics

What do you do succession planning? How do you effectively establish what makes a person "right" for management? We'll be looking at how to establish the core competencies of the positions and how to incorporate all we've learned so far into a meaningful process for succession planning.

The Intention

When you begin the selection process, like a good baseball coach, you want to look for the inherent talents and strengths of an individual. Who in your organization do people go to for information, for support, and for positive reinforcement? Who do you believe supports you and the efforts of the company? Choosing more than one is wise as people do leave and some just don't want to manage others.

Session Structure and Process

When you have determined your first list of potential leaders, check to see if there are others outside your organization that might also be worth cultivating. It is better to have a large list to begin than a very small list that becomes extinct rapidly. This is one of the first pitfalls that face managers in succession planning – too small a list. If the list is only one person then you may need to consider future hires with the focus on leadership.

Planning

The second step after the list building is to consider the core competencies, skills and experience required for the job of leading your organization. This is very important. Many managers draw up the list from top performers but then realize later (usually after the promotion) that this was not the right person; that they lack necessary skills or competencies for this level. The "Peter Prinicple" is an old adage that means someone has finally risen to a level of incompetence. Not their fault but certainly a lack of understanding and/or training from the people that

132

promoted them. People must not only have the desire to lead the organization; they must also have the skills and knowledge.

Beginning

Establishing these core competencies, skills and experience start with a review of what it takes for <u>you</u> to do your job. If you feel you cannot be objective, consider working with a coach or another peer to look at your strengths and weaknesses. The following questions will help you do your evaluation; feel free to add more!

1. How many years experience do I have? How many are really *relevant* to managing this group?
2. What experience or skill do I use most often as a manager of this organization? *Consider whether you need technical skills, accounting background, strong HR, legal, or operations.* How much of these do you need? *Do you need to be very strong or just general understanding?*
3. What skills or experience would help me be even more effective in this job?
4. What core competencies do I use on a daily basis that supports this job? *For instance you might consider the following:*

1. Customer Focus	8. Building Effective Teams
2. Command Skills	9. Developing Direct Reports
3. Intellectual Horsepower	10. Learning on the Fly
4. Integrity and Trust	11. Organizational Agility
5. Business Acumen	12. Problem Solving
6. Functional/Technical Skills	13. Priority Setting
7. Dealing with Ambiguity	14. Drive for Results

For a more complete list, you may want to check out Lominger[©] Core Competencies. Your HR department may have a set of these cards and instructions on how to use them.[3] The list above is a good start and to make this effective, I would not worry too much about whether something is a skill, experience or core competency. Brainstorm just to develop a list that speaks to the job that needs to be done. The more detailed the list the more effective your succession planning would be.

5. Now consider what you wish you had. What would make your job easier if you were better at it? *One of the great things about this activity is that while you are training your succession list, you can participate as well! It will only make you stronger when you move up!*

---

[3] Lominger[©] is available through www.lominger.com

6. The last piece is to think of who you would want to do your job if you had to be out of the office for an extended period. What if a big decision came up during your vacation or conference? Who would make the best decisions in your absence? Why? What gives you that level of confidence? Who do you trust most in your absence? Why? Check yourself on these answers. Are they good business reasons or are they purely ego?

7. In many large corporations there is a fear of managers naming their own replacements for fear they would recommend someone who was less effective at their job than themselves. While this may be an issue, how would that support you as you move up? Would you want to have management looking back and questioning your decision process when your suggested replacement begins to fail? Do you want to move forward or be continually looking at your back? Do you want to build new and better or do you want the executive staff looking at your decisions and wondering if you are going to make another mistake? When we allow ego to keep us from making the best decisions for the overall good of the organization, we limit our success.

Your investment is in the company and the company has an investment in you. Making good solid decisions that support the growth and prosperity of the business is critical to all your actions and evaluations.

The Process

Now that your lists are made, let's organize them in a meaningful way.

Making a matrix of names and core competencies, we'll use this to evaluate the top 5 or more candidates. The matrix might look like this:

Core Competencies/Skills/Experience	Joe	Marsha	Tom
1. Customer Focus	1	2	1
2. Command Skills	3	1	2
3. Intellectual Horsepower	2	2	3
4. Integrity and Trust	2	3	4
5. Business Acumen	4	3	4
6. Functional/Technical Skills	1	2	1
7. Dealing with Ambiguity	5	4	5
8. Building Effective Teams	3	1	5
9. Developing Direct Reports	3	1	5
10. Learning on the Fly	1	3	1
11. Organizational Agility	4	4	5
12. Problem Solving	1	1	1
13. Priority Setting	3	1	1
14. Drive for Results	5	1	1

Key:
1 = very strong, needs no training
2 = strong, some coaching
3 = average, needs training and experience
4 = not observable
5 = overused or definable weakness

This is a sample. Your list might be much larger and your key may be different. What we are working toward is a quick evaluation tool to determine who stays on your list and what will then be required to get them up to speed.

You will use this list to begin conversations with your supervisor. One of the ways to approach this is just to be honest. Here's an example with George as your supervisor:

Example:
"George, one of the things that are important to me is to create a couple of successors. You know that I want to move up in the organization some day. I want you to feel comfortable in recommending me if the right position comes up in our company. So one of the things that I have done is gone through my team and evaluated their potential for management.

"The first step I took was to look at what it takes to get the job done. I'd like for you to look at the list I drew up and see if there is anything you would add or perhaps delete."

Show George the list and discuss various aspects of your choices. Ask for his input.

Now show him the matrix. If he wanted to add some things, add them immediately to your matrix or tell him you'll add them later and get his feedback on the new evaluation. For now, show him your thoughts on the people. Who would he add to the list? What would make them a good candidate in his mind? What scores would he give them against the list? Is he in agreement with the scores you have given people on the list?

When the conversation ends, let him know you'll make the changes and give him a copy. Let him know that you will also be developing a training plan for enhancing people on the list. If dollars are short in the training budget, you may need to be creative but the thought that you have put into this discussion just might buy you an increased training budget. You can almost guarantee that George hasn't made such a list! This is also a good sanity check against both your performance appraisals and also your compensation for the employees. (This sanity check is for your reference only at this time, not with your manager.)

Active Learning Tools

Once you have made your manager aware of your efforts and some form of approval, begin to look for opportunities to bring these key people into the business at another level. Here are some ideas for growing their skills that shouldn't hit the budget too hard (or not at all.)

1. Consider using a roundtable format to discuss problems in the area and have them help you determine new methodologies and process. Be sure that you are asking questions that make them think about the "business needs" (the larger picture.) This creates a good opportunity to see how much they realize about the business and the effect the department has on the rest of the organization.

2. Consider giving each one of them a project to develop a new process. Tell them that it may not be implemented in full but you would like to see their thought process and how they would go about the effort. You are looking for business awareness, people skills, implementation and project management skills. You are also looking for how well they can go from A-Z and whether they skip important points. And best yet, do they even realize whether those points are important? It is best if the project has real meaning and can be implemented if they come up with great new ideas. *No one likes to do a lot of work for nothing!*

3. Ask them to mentor new employees and build a mentoring plan. The plan can be built as a group or individually but the mentoring should be done individually. Be sure that part of the plan is to test or measure success. Every manager needs to know how to do this and why it's important. You are looking for how well they can manage process, projects and people in this exercise. Can they develop direct reports? Are they good at building teams? How well can they coach?

Each of these will offer you many coaching opportunities. Hold the intention that this is building their strengths and giving *you* a way to be more successful and move on to great things!

Note: It might not be wise to tell these candidates that you are thinking of moving on until there is an obvious position available. We are building skills not a competitive environment or a chance for concern over coming change.

I do not tell anyone they are on the succession list until I am sure that they are really stepping up to the plate. I also do not want to get their hopes up if my supervisor/executive doesn't buy off on them. You also want to see if they develop because they love a challenge or if they only get excited when the carrot is visible. You know as a manager that most of what needs to be done does not have a reward at the end so having people on the list, who only want the reward, won't give you the results you need.

Consider Options

Continue to evaluate all your staff even after the list is made. There have been times when someone pops up that I hadn't even considered. Sometimes it's because they see the extra attention paid to the ones on the list and they really want to participate. Other times they appear because they just got their act together and feel like it's time for more. Either way, keep your eyes open!

Apply the information to the real world

Whenever you are coaching or asking for projects, be sure that your potential successors are looking at the big picture. How does what they do affect the larger organization? Do they know who their customers are? Internal and external? Do they see the impact of what they are doing on their team members? Are they always thinking of ways to save the company time and money? If they are focused on these things, it will show up in many ways. You will notice the change in your organization and so will your boss. When it comes time to be promoted, choosing your successor will be an easy sale (although with such great choices it may be hard to choose!)

In Conclusion

Creating an effective succession plan can never start too early. In some organizations, due to the youth or lack of experience in the staff, it may take years to develop the appropriate leadership. Learning to coach and mentor the next and future level of management will always be a critical factor for your career and the organization's ultimate success.

Start today with your list and matrix. Consider what you wish you had known when you were first promoted and then develop ways to be sure that your successor will have the necessary abilities. How you *leave* a job is as important as how you *do* a job while you are there. As you climb the executive ladder, it is nicer to have people cheering behind you rather than jeering!

Integration Scenario:

Candace has her eye on the new department that has been discussed in the senior management meetings. She has been making good suggestions about its role in the organization and how it can improve customer service and delivery. She sees success around the corner. However, she knows that her current position is equally critical. Although she and her boss have not talked about promotion at this point, she knows that he would see a loss to his organization if she moved over. A hole in his organization would not encourage him to refer her into the new department.

Candace decides to be proactive and build a succession plan. She knows the new department will not start until the Board approves it next quarter at the annual meeting so she has 90-120 days to put her plan in action.

Candace builds a list of core competencies and skills she feels are important to her job. Over lunch she asks her boss what other skills he would consider are necessary for her. Bob raises his eyebrow and asks, "What's this all about? Are you worried about your raise or do you want some more training?"

Candace laughs and says, "Leave it to you, Bob, it's always about money! Seriously, that's not it. I'm looking at developing a few of my people for succession planning. Someday, I AM going to hit you up for a promotion and I want to be sure that you will have qualified candidates to choose from."

Bob replies, "What do you have in mind?"

"I'd like for you to consider these core competencies in two lights. First, what you currently expect of me and a future replacement. Second, what else would you like to see? Maybe some areas that I could add to my current repertoire or that you feel will be important in the future."

"My next step will then be to evaluate my current team on these various competencies and skills. I'll be looking for the strongest candidates. You know the ones with the most potential. I'll be asking you to look at the list and add or subtract based on your perception of the individuals. After all, if you don't see an individual working for you it wouldn't be valuable to start them down the path. Although, I'm quite sure with a company of our size, there would be additional opportunities outside of our organization. Even if they never assume a management role they will make better team players, don't you think?" Candace explains.

"Hmmm, I see what you mean. That's actually quite a good plan. I'll look forward to seeing your list. What will you do after the list of people is made?" Bob asks.

"I'm going to evaluate where they are strongest and weakest against each of these core competencies. For instance, Janice is one of the people I'm pretty sure I'll have on the list. She is a great mentor and coach to new people so she'll rate high in that category. However, I've never had the opportunity to test her political savvy with other people outside the department. So to start with, I'll rate her low for a "wait and see" and to look for training opportunities. As those situations come up I'll be evaluating her and will change the score when I see real improvement. That's why your opinion of both this list of skills and competencies *and* the list of people is critical.

"There will be times when I'll ask you to let them sit on non-confidential business meetings or to replace me on small projects so that I can get a good read on how sharp they are at different or new experiences. This is something I want to do to test them without making an issue of my reasons. I'll want your feedback and that of other managers. Objective feedback will be very important to the success of the plan." Candace elaborates.

Bob nods, "I like it. I really like it. It makes me think we need to do more of this across the company. I don't think I've seen anything like this. When do you think you'll have the list of people ready?"

Candace replies, "I've got a rough list but it wasn't based on these competencies. So now I'll sit down and run it through this list with your additions. I should have it done by Monday. I think it will help to review it this weekend over a quiet moment. I can show it to you after our conference call on Monday if you'd like."
Bob nods. "Actually, I'd like to have a copy of the core competencies to review. How much would I set back the time table if I made more changes and additions?"

"Not much." Candace says, "I'll still go ahead with my plan and then Monday we can just talk through the changes and the people, if you have time. I think this should be a co-creative process, don't you?"

"Indeed. Especially since I know you're going to hit me up for training money and a promotion some day soon!" Bob chuckles.

"I'll try not to dip into your wallet too much." Candace smiles, "I really do think a lot of this will be OJT (on the job training.) Experiential learning is always better for adults and coaching doesn't cost anything but my time."

"Candace, I'm really pleased with this. This took a lot of effort and thought. It's an example of *why I'm probably going to be forced to promote you some day.*" Bob smiles and winks.

"Thanks. That means a lot to me. I appreciate you for being open to this."

Lessons Learned:

1. What did you find challenging in this lesson?

2. How much succession planning does your organization currently do?

3. How could you introduce the process into your organization and gain buy-in?

4. If you are not currently in a management or supervisory position, how could you effectively use this lesson to increase your chances of success?

5. What core competencies would be valuable to you in your current job?

6. What core competencies would you add in order to do an excellent job in your supervisor's position? (NOTE: I used the word "excellent" because ultimately when you are promoted, you want to excel in your new position!)

7. How many people do you feel are ready to be on the succession list in your organization?

Chapter 7

Communicating Effectively

You've heard the old adage, "work smarter, not harder?" Who hasn't? When we begin to effectively communicate with intention and purpose, our jobs get easier, more fun and the old adage takes care of itself. But how can you make communication easier and more productive? Especially as a manager, many of us have had times when we would just not have any conversation. Why can't people just get the picture and do their work? Why do I have to manage them through the maze?

If you are in a management position now (and I assume you are or wish to be if you are reading this book,) then you have probably had moments when these thoughts have crossed your mind. They are generally loudest when you have to do a performance review or the dreaded PIP (Performance Improvement Process) with an employee. Some of these can send even the best manager running to hide. But how can you create a better scenario? How can you get your employees to see the big picture without having to continually draw the picture? How can get them so excited, motivated, and aligned with your organizational goals that you only have to steer the ship?

Does this sound too good to be true?

Communication becomes easier and more effective when you know some of the key ingredients. When *you* become more fluent in these powerful communication ingredients you'll find you have better results, happier employees and lower blood pressure.

A Recipe for Successful Communication

40% positive attitude = Believe that the other person has something valuable to say!
30% present = focus and be fully attentive to the discussion at hand! (not easy in today's electronic media blitz – cell phones, pagers, computers, etc.)
30% ASK more than Tell = learning to use *effective* questioning techniques and laser precision in your communication will have you working less and enjoying communication more!

The Basics

Effective Questions are a concept that will not be new to you. All good communications classes spend time on them but we'll explore them in a new context here. You recognize effective questions by the way you *feel* after the conversation. If you have ever had a really great *dialogue* with someone (a truly outstanding communicator) think of the questions they asked you. How thought provoking were the questions? How did you have to answer them? How did they build off *your* answers with *more* questions? Where did that take you in the conversation? How rewarding did you find the exchange? What were the questions that created such a deep dialogue?

In the paragraph above, I just asked you a number of effective questions. It's the beginning a truly effective communication. So let's take some time to get underneath the process.

Structure of Effective Questions

1. The structure of an effective question begins with an open-ended question. You've heard of that before, I'm sure. It's a question that *cannot* be answered with a one-word answer. It demands a full and thoughtful answer. If you ask a really *great* effective question, you may find people will ask for time to think about the answer. Honor the request and pat yourself on the back! It was a really *great* question. Get ready for a really good answer that will build into a powerful dialogue.

2. The second part of an effective question is where it leads the other person. In an effective question you want to *create a new awareness*. The focus of your question will be the focus of their answer. In a book called, Getting to the Heart of Change, by Ed Oakley and Doug Krug, they spend time discussing the impact of a concept called *forward focus*. This is a solutions based orientation. To

make it simple and direct for our discussion purposes, it keeps the conversation on "What can be done to be successful?" This is the type of question that will *energize* you and your employee.

If you ask questions that are backward focused you will leave feeling drained and know that you did not get the results you want. What's important about creating the right focus? What's important to you as a manager? Do you want to hear their excuses or get to the solution? It's a choice we make as managers on a daily basis. If you are hearing excuses, you are asking the wrong questions. The value of the answer is dependent in large part on the quality of the question.

3. The last part of the equation is the *intention* you hold as you ask the question.

   o When *you are open* to learning and developing as a manager
   o When you are open to *creating* a learning environment for your employee
   o When you want someone to create solutions and get better results
   o When you wish to develop stronger leaders and change agents in your organization…

Then you will consciously choose to ask

effective questions.

It is almost impossible to ask an ineffective question when you hold all three of these principles together at the same time.

1. **Open-ended** – request for more information

2. **Focus** - Solution based, looking for resolution and success
3. **Positive Intention** – the other person has value and you want to hear what they have to say.

Open-Ended

- Starting with *WHAT and HOW* will create an open-ended question.
- While it is possible to create an open dialogue with other directives, these will create a faster result and better chances for success.

Focus

What is it you really want to learn from the employee, peer or management? Questions like:
- What does success look like?
- How would you define an effective strategy in this situation?
- What would be the benefit to us (you) if we created a different solution?
- What would that solution have to have to change the current situation?
- What would "X" have to be to achieve "Y?"

Look at these questions carefully. What do you notice about the answers you would have to give? *Solutions, right?* Now notice that you are directing the other person by the quality of these questions. Better yet, you are getting *very valuable* information that you can use to work with them in a positive and meaningful way.

The Intention of working together

Intention is not always a conscious thought for most of us in the workforce. We are hammering through our days with a loaded schedule, reams of e-mail and a steady stream of phone-mail. We are in react mode more than we are aware.

The key to truly effective communication is being aware of how open you are to the other person. If you move into the conversation with attachment to what is going to be said (on both sides,) and expect a specific outcome, you will find your conversations very strained and find resistance at every turn.

Remember your last three conversations:
- Were they effective?
- Did you get a specific outcome?
- Did you feel they were a dialogue or a discussion?
- Did you feel that the person would whole-heartedly support your outcome? Or did you feel resistance?

Every conversation has an opportunity hidden in it. It has the ability to strengthen our relationships, our support structure, our knowledge and our team's ability to grow and develop in meaningful ways. Sound like a heavy responsibility? Yes, it can be. *It is also the key to real leadership and success.*

What these conversations can be are dialogues for progress. Have you noticed the reference to dialogue vs. discussion? Discussion has the same root word as percussion. It means to break apart. Dialogue is two coming together for the

purpose of exchange. Interesting concept? Very
from our normal exchanges, isn't it?

This does not mean that you do not set direction and
outcomes for your teams. It *does* mean that you allow space
for their opinions and questions. It *does* mean that they may
have better, faster, more effective ways to get to your
outcome if you hold the intention for excellence and
respect. Even poor performers will shift to a more effective
behavior if you ask for *their* best methods.

Use active learning tools

In order to reach mastery of effective questions, begin to
practice them throughout your workday and at home. Make
a list of questions (five or six, at first) that will support you
in creating a positive focus. Look at them in relationship to
the questions in the list below. I have taken some of the
questions from this lesson as well as some of my favorites
over the years to give you a starting point. Grade these for
yourself. Would they work for you in your communication
with others? How could you change them to meet your style
and personality and still hold the same focus and intention?
Feel free to play with them. Your success is important to
me.

1. What is the best way to reach this goal?
2. What strengths can we build on to make this project
   more successful?
3. What can we do better or differently?
4. What would you like to see happen here?
5. How could we meet our goal in less time?
6. What does success look like?

7. How would you define an effective strategy in this situation?
8. What would be the benefit to us (you) if we created a different solution?
9. What would that solution have to have to change the current situation?
10. What would "X" have to be to achieve "Y?"
11. What's important to you?
12. What would support you best in this situation?
13. How could I support you?
14. What could you do to see yourself as a top performer?
15. How do you see yourself as a leader of this team?
16. What would make our department number one?

In Conclusion

Asking will make your job easier <u>if</u> you ask truly effective questions. You will notice that everyone with whom you talk will be much more responsive and amenable to your suggestions because you have:

- Created positive focus
- Honored them by asking for their opinions with positive intention
- Listened attentively
- Built on their answers and suggestions
- And proven to be an *excellent communicator!*

If you wish to relieve the stress points in your life, try asking more effective questions. You will find you don't have to work as hard. People will be willing to help you achieve your goals and you just might start having some fun!

Integration Scenario

These two scenarios will help you to see the effect of intention and the use of effective questions.

Bob has been a manager for a year now. He has been trained on performance appraisals, knows the procedures and the requirements but consistently turns them in late. His employees are unhappy and do not feel valued. You have heard numerous complaints and escalations. What do you do?

Scenario One: *Bob enters your office.*

You: Bob, I've noticed on the HR report that you have several late reviews again. What's happening?

Bob: I don't know. There's a lot going on right now. We have several projects that need my consistent attention and these just really take a long time to write up. Then I have to sit down with each person to discuss it. I just don't have time.

You: Bob, I appreciate the attention you are giving the projects right now, however this is a critical part of your job. You have to get these done. People's salaries and development plans depend on timely input from you.

Bob: I know, I know. I'll get it done. I'll focus on it this weekend and get them to you by next Friday.

Sound familiar? Can you relate to Bob? To the manager? To both? Most of us have been on either side of that table at one point in our careers. But let's really look at this. While the manager got what he wants – the reports done by a certain date and commitment to doing it – what's the quality? Is Bob going to do a truly effective job in writing these? Delivering them? How are Bob's people going to feel? It will be done but what kind of feedback are the employees really going to get?

Scenario Two:

Mgr: Bob, I noticed the HR report this morning and we've got some late reviews. What's happening on yours?

Bob: I know, I know, I've been very busy with the projects.

Mgr: I know that's true. (pause and breathe) Bob, it's important to me that we let our folks know that they are valuable to us. What's important to you?

Bob: Right now getting these projects in on schedule.

Mgr: That is very important and you've got a really good team that is working very hard.

Bob: Yeah, everybody's putting in extra effort right now.

Mgr: That's so critical for our company. When push comes to shove these guys get the work done.

Bob: Yeah, it's not always easy.

Mgr: What do you think is important to them?

Bob: Getting these projects put to bed and breathing for a while.

Mgr (chuckling): Agreed. What else do you think is important to them?

Bob: Feeling successful and doing a good job.

Mgr: What else?

Bob: Being recognized for all their hard work.

Mgr: I think that's true for all of us. (Pause) Sometimes in the crush of business that feeling of success and doing a good job gets lost, don't you think?

Bob: Yes, I do. I've felt that way myself sometimes.

Mgr: How important is it to you for me to let you know that you are appreciated and valued as an employee?

Bob: Very important. It makes me feel better about what I'm doing and why.

Mgr: I believe that also and it's tough for me sometimes to find the time to recognize the good work you do. There are always pressures. But it is your expectation that I pay attention and make sure you get that recognition. You expect it to be informal and <u>formal</u>. You expect it to show up in your evaluation and your raise, right? (Said with a smile.)

Bob: I get it. This is your oh so subtle way of telling me that the evaluations for my guys is important to them. (Shaking his head and grimacing.)

Mgr: Yes, it is my way. What's the impact if we don't give time to the evaluations?

Bob: Well...they won't get their raises or promotions and they may get mad and leave. I sure can't afford that.

Mgr: You're right none of us can afford to lose good people. The process demands our attention to the evaluations as a way to make sure that we acknowledge our employees and can support their raises and bonuses. Your team has worked too hard not to have the recognition. The bad part for you is the cycle time puts it at a very busy time for you. It's not fair...but it would be <u>less</u> fair not to get the raises and evaluations in for your team.

158

Bob: Yeah. I'd hate to only be able to give them a cost of living raise when they've worked so hard.

Mgr: You really understand what I'm saying and I appreciate how quickly you grasp the importance of this. What do you think is doable?

Bob: Look, I need to work late each night this week anyway. It's not that I'm doing any programming but I want to be here to support the guys. I'll work on the evaluations each night and this weekend. I think I can have them to you by Monday close of business at the latest. If I'm not on schedule with that I'll let you know. It means walking around the floor less but they'll know I'm here.

Mgr: Bob, that's better than I hoped for with your schedule. I'll tell HR and Accounting that we need the extra time. It would help me if we could quickly review your first thoughts on your team and the kind of raises you were hoping to give them. That way I can begin preparing the budget and give you a head's up if there will be any problems. How does that work for you?

The key to this process is developing the understanding that it is not punitive, make work. Establishing a link between what is important to you, to your employee and to their team, helps them leap to the right conclusions and <u>own</u> the situation. Whenever possible you should offer support while maintaining their accountability. Notice that the Manager never used the "we" scenario. He kept the ball firmly placed in Bob's court while helping him grasp what needed to be done. Once Bob took responsibility the Manager supported him in other ways.

Notice the use of effective questions that lead Bob to deeper understanding. Changing behaviors for both others and ourselves is challenging at times. The key is to create an opportunity to learn and grow in your exchanges so that you will not have to revisit them as often. Bob and his manager may need one or two more dialogues but they will be shorter and more effective each time because Bob has now *internalized* the need to get appraisals done on time. He also realizes how important the later dialogue will be with his employees. So rather than haphazardly doing the reviews, he'll give more thought to the real message he wants to deliver.

Lessons Learned

1. What happened that was significant in this dialogue?

2. Does Bob have a better understanding of how his job impacts the lives and futures of others?

3. Will he put more thought and effort into their creation and delivery?

4. What was the intention of the manager in both scenarios?

5. How did it affect the outcome in both conversations?

6. Where can you use effective questions?

7. What outcomes would change with their use?

8. How would the outcomes change?

9. How would your employees (or managers) react if they were asked effective questions?

Write 5 effective questions and then test them on some friends, family or colleagues. Evaluate how they answered. Did you receive thoughtful answers and/or solutions?

How could you make the questions more effective?

Try again. *Remember, a really powerful effective question will take a while to formulate an answer and the answer will be well worth waiting for!*

Chapter 8

Developing Process Easily

Process is a great way to take away excuses in your organization. Getting people involved in creating the process creates buy-in. Add to this equation a solid set of expectations and watch your team excel.

The Basics

So often when I begin work with organizations I will hear two reasons for frustration. One is lack of role/responsibility definition and the second is lack of process definition. Now in fairness if the process isn't defined it's very hard to assign roles and responsibilities. Creating process definition can be easier than you think. The exercise presented here is fun, positive and creates tremendous buy-in as everyone can participate. It can be a great teambuilding exercise if done with the right intention.

The Intention

Start with a clear expectation. What does success look like for your organization? What outcomes do you expect your people to meet and in what timeframe? Set the intention that they can meet these consistently if you have a solid process. Further that intention with the idea that they already *know how to do their job* but may not have thought through the process... *until now!* It is also very helpful for you and your team to hold the perceptions that together, you can create a better process (even if it's the same one but now it's documented!) and that it will be *fun!* (I know that's a no-no word but I can't help using it. FUN is a good thing...even in business!)

Session Structure and Process

This process is highly interactive and active. Be ready to let people get noisy and move around freely.

Pre-session Planning

- Set your expectations. Have them written down on a flipchart and practice articulating them effectively. Consider recording yourself to review whether you are hitting all the points.
- Supplies:
  - o Flipchart
  - o Lots of colored markers

o Felt tip pens with heavy ink (Sharpies® are great)
o Lots of Post-It Notes® (multi-color is fine but may be distracting so consider only one color for this exercise)
o Butcher Paper or the brown postal paper rolls (in desperation you can use the white backs of wrapping paper. Just be sure that the post-its are visible on whatever paper you choose.)
o Masking tape or painter's blue tape so you don't ruin walls
o Round dots with sticky backs in at least 4 different colors.

Session Opening

Let people know that you are going to be having a *fun* session. If you can hold this off-site, great, if not, see if you can allow casual attire. It will help create a more dynamic atmosphere.

Prepare the room by attaching the butcher paper around the outside walls with the top of the paper just barely above the top of average height. You want to be able to accommodate everyone in your group so that they can attach their sticky notes to the butcher paper with ease.

Give each person a set of Post-It Notes®, just one stack per person (not the whole pack!) Have a felt tip pen for each person.

Terah Stearns

Explain the process of working together

Now spend time talking about your expectations.

Example:
"I've heard from many of you that our XYZ process needs to be defined or documented or that roles need to be more clearly defined. I've got a fun exercise today for us to see what that process looks like and capture it together."

"In front of each of you is (are) a pen and some notepads. We'll be using them today to analyze our process. Before we begin, I want to review our goals for this department to be clear that we know what success looks like and make sure that the process we define together is truly effective. After all, if we want to get to San Jose we don't want to build a map to St. Louis!"

(After reviewing the goals)

"I made a quick breakdown of the major categories of work we do in this department. Would you agree with the 5 (or two or three...) that I have up here? Would you do different categories or add to the list? (Allow them to help you set the categories. An example might be packaging, shipping, loading, etc.)"

"Okay, now that we have the main groups of work, let's begin looking at tasks. Using the notepads in front of you I want you to put only one <u>task</u> per note. (Example) So just for packaging you will have several tasks from receiving merchandise, to sizing box, checking label accuracy, etc. Start with the tasks that you are directly responsible for and

166

then branch out to other areas. Even though you aren't in packaging you can add shipping and loading tasks. We're looking for a composite of all tasks. "

"Don't worry about having it all down. Others will think of anything you might miss and we're going to be refining this process as we go to other exercises. (NOTE: this allows the detail oriented people to feel comfortable with the task.)

Now as they begin writing tasks on the notepads walk around and make sure there is only one task per note and that people are not stuck. Sometimes it helps to offer another suggestion or two to get them started.

Use active learning tools

While they are writing out tasks, go to the butcher paper and block out sections for each of the main categories that they have agreed upon. Give them about 10 minutes to write as many tasks as they can. Once the tasks are written out ask them to go and put their Post-It Notes® on the appropriate section of the butcher paper (in other words, each note should have one task relating to a category written on the butcher paper.) Tell them not to worry about order at this point, just make sure the right task gets into the right category.

This causes some pretty noisy activity but that in itself creates additional energy and the exchange is very healthy. This will look something like the picture below when it is completed (only not as neat!)

Focus the discussion

Now break them into groups. It is helpful to have people from various categories (like shipping, packaging, etc.) working on the same team. This gives some additional feedback from different groups and some very objective opinions as to rethinking the process. You will have as many groups as you have primary categories. If you had three major categories, as I've used in the examples, then you'll have three groups; more categories mean more groups.

Now ask each group to take one category. Have teams move to the butcher paper (with their Post-It Notes® and felt tip pens) and do the following things:

- *Remove duplication (some tasks may be worded differently but the same idea)*
- *If some duplication has more than one task on the note, rewrite the tasks <u>one per note.</u>*
- *Now have them order the tasks in sequence of events. What comes first, second, etc.?*
- *If some tasks need to be described in more detail put a sticky note with a big symbol or the word MORE on it or use a bright color marker to signify more. Ask them not to elaborate yet. We will do this soon. (In the diagram below the yellow boxes are for more information.)*
- *The last part is to look for sub-categories. For instance, in packaging, there may be a sub-category for box inventory re-supply or ordering shipping inventory.*

168

What we are looking for here is to see if there is additional ways to break down the process into meaningful components. You do not have to ask them to do this but if they are getting lost in the process, this will be your cue to help them sort in a more logical order.

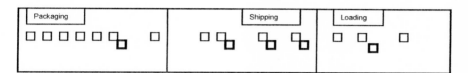

Now that it is organized and the areas for additional information have been noted it's time to ask them to fill in the blanks. Have them start with the notes that ask for more information. Use different color sticky notes or a different marker color to note the new tasks. Ask them to put the new notes in order along with the other sticky notes.

What will come up during this part of the session are tasks that must be done simultaneously or by different divisions and feed into the process. That's where other colors of Post-It Notes® will help. Ask them to identify these items and put them underneath or beside the appropriate note and mark them (for example: 1A, 1B.) This will help later in determining sequence and dependencies.

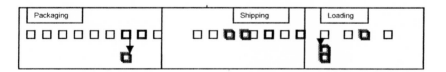

Options

Now switch the groups around. Have packaging go to loading, loading go to shipping, and shipping will then go to packaging.

Have them walk through the process that the other team decided. Have them evaluate whether it makes sense to them. Have them check to see if anything is missing and add it in. This will not take more than 10 minutes and you can decide whether you want to do another round or feel that it is complete.

The next step is to test for pain. Give each group a page of the color dots. I love to get bright colors like blue, red, yellow, and green. Ask the group to now go through and put dots above the sticky notes for the following categories:

- A yellow dot on any area that is slowing down the process. (In the diagram as a triangle.)
- A red dot where the process is painful or really gets stopped. (In the diagram as a circle.)
- A green dot for areas where the system works amazingly well. (In the diagram as a star.)

- A blue dot for areas where they are very dependent on others. (In the diagram as a circle with an X.)

This makes the board pretty wild looking. In the example I am only highlighting a couple to make a point.

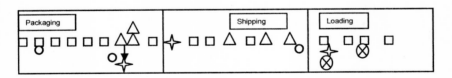

You may at this point ask them to go back to work and tell them you will resume next week or tomorrow as this is a good stopping point.

If you can continue, the next steps are to facilitate discussion around the various dots. Here's what you are looking for in the process:

• What makes the green dots work so well? Get specific in terms of process, tools, people, etc. that make this part of process so efficient.

• What slows down the process on the yellow dots? What ideas do they have to speed it up? *If their answers are all about certain people or departments, make these notes and tell them that you will look for ways to bring the process discussion to that department. Make sure that you ask your team <u>what they can do to improve or adapt for the deficiencies of the other department?</u> There are always going to be times when you cannot budge the other person. What can you do to work ahead or around their issues?*

• On the blue dots, what dependencies are working well? What makes them work so well? Are there areas where these same ideas could be used in other parts of the process? <u>Are there ways to recognize excellent support in these areas of dependency?</u> *(One of the best ways to get more support is to recognize the other fellow! Example: one department showed up one day about 15 minutes before lunch with two armloads of pizza for the other crew! Just to say thanks for their support and helping their department be so successful. Talk about getting excellent service! Besides, the team giving the pizzas loved surprising the other department and made for real camaraderie.)*

• Now for the red dots. This is where you want to get outside the box!

1. Allow your team to tell you what makes it so painful. HEAR THEM! Capture their issues on a flipchart. Make sure you don't filter it. Let them vent. This is amazingly cathartic and will help them get more creative about the solutions later.
2. Ask them what they would most like to do to improve the process. If they are stuck, use brainstorming techniques. Ask them what they would do if there was "no gravity." ("No gravity" means take any limitations away to get them started. Not enough money, say, "What if we had an infinite budget?" Then ask the opposite, "What would we do if we had NO money?") Get them to brainstorm on both sides of the topic. This will help them create more options than looking only at the way things are today.
3. Consider breaking them back into groups to see who can come up with the best options for this problem. Then have them report back to the group. The group can then decide which idea will work best or decide to test the top two ideas.
4. If the pain is caused by another organization, get as many ideas as possible and then ask for a small key group to volunteer to meet with you and representatives of the other organization to come to some new process steps. *You will want to allow the other group to have a similar opportunity to brainstorm ideas.*

As you come to decisions with new steps to the process ask members of the group to add sticky notes to the butcher paper.

Apply the information to the real world

Now ask the group to walk through the process with several real world examples. One with a problem, others that have minor challenges and at least one that is easy. This allows the group to see whether the process works and is complete. Have them add sticky notes as needed.

The very last step is to tag who or what position owns the tasks, who they hand off to and how long each task should take. Make notes under the sticky notes to be clear on accountability.

Closing

When the task is complete (for the day,) put masking tape on the top of each sticky note to ensure that it does not fall off. You can even take the time to number them but I find the masking or painter's tape to be valuable. You can then roll up the butcher paper and take it to your office for transcription.

Finally, bring closure to the session by:
- asking for feedback,
- drawing conclusions,
- identifying next steps,
- Or simply sharing information about the experience of the session.

Always close the session by *thanking them* for being so open to exploring more effective ways to work with their team and you.

In Conclusion

When your staff supports you in preparing process, many excuses disappear. Process, or lack thereof, is always a big excuse. It is an easy meeting to facilitate and staff feel terrific buy-in on several issues; first, because they are heard; second, because they participate in the process development. Using this interactive process can also help you to truly understand where your staff is limited and where they can excel. This will also help you in negotiating with other departments on better handoffs and a more streamlined operation.

Integration Scenario:

Terry had just done a few one-on-one meetings with his staff. He found that there seemed to be some stress in the programming groups. The constant comments seemed to relate to a lack of coordination and more than one person had commented on roles and responsibilities. Terry's group had completed several significant projects in the past and he had assumed that this new roll-out would be no different. However, the tension in the office was higher than normal and these comments created some concern. Rather than waiting until there was a time crunch or more significant issues, he decided to take a day for an off-site.

Pulling out his notes for process development, he planned his meeting. First he cleared with the V.P. that he was going to use some of his budget dollars for the meeting and alerted his fellow directors that his staff would be off-site for a day, he began to make his shopping list. He then sent a note to staff and invited them to the meeting to discuss project delivery success. He left the invitation vague to keep the staff curious and to come with an open mind.

Terry spent an hour considering what he had heard about the issues of coordination and job responsibilities. He built his objectives for the session off of the employee comments.

The day of the session, Terry was at the conference center early. He set up the flip chart with objectives and passed out yellow Post-It Notes® and felt tip pens for each seat. He then taped the butcher paper up on the wall. Using his colored markers he wrote the four categories for the programming process: project management, development, quality assurance, and customer service. He took the extra table at the front of the room to lay out the additional supplies. He was well prepared and relaxed as the first of his employees walked in. He joined them for coffee and juice and chatted amiably until time for the session to begin.

"Welcome and thanks for joining me today. Recently, I set down to talk with a few of you for my quarterly one-on-one meetings. Before I got too far into the process it sounded like we were beginning to have some issues with the new project. Because I had heard the same thing for a majority of the people I spoke with, I frankly, jumped to a conclusion. I decided it might be worth a group meeting to iron out how we want to proceed on this project and develop clear roles and responsibilities.

"Am I too far off track or do you agree that our old way of working may not fit this project as well as others?" Terry asked the group.

There was general agreement and no one stated disagreement so Terry proceeded. "As you all know this is an important project for the company and I know the timeline has been extended because there is still some general miscommunication about what the executives want the customer management system to do. However, once they have made that decision, then it's up to us to make it successful and bug-free, right?"

There was full agreement and a few general comments about how long it was taking the execs to make up there mind. Terry smiled and continued, "Then our topic today is to build a seamless process and define who owns what and what our dependencies are. For the most part we know this. We've made it work in the past but the process I've put together for today will help us refine it quickly and even test it against various scenarios. Are you game?"

Again, full agreement and some curious looks accompanied his question.

"In front of you is a stack of Post-It Notes® and a felt tip pen. What I want you to do is break down your job and the project into tasks. One task per Post-It Note®. Write as many as you can think of and don't worry about duplicating what others may have written, we'll take care of that later. For now just think of as many tasks as possible. I'll give you about 10 minutes and you just do a brain-dump on the sticky notes." Terry instructed.

When the 10 minutes was up, Terry asked if anyone needed a little more time. One or two people asked for another minute. Terry agreed. Calling time a minute later, Terry pointed to the butcher paper. "Now to help you sort through these tasks, consider these four categories. I felt these were major categories of work in our department. Do you feel that there is something else that should be up there?"

A suggestion to add "marketing interface" raised some discussion with the group and was decided that it was a major category. Terry added that to the butcher paper.
"Now what I want you to do is put your Post-It Notes® under each category that applies. Don't worry about order yet, just get them up there. If you see some duplication, put you Post-It Note® with the other one and we'll evaluate later." Terry stood back and allowed the team to gather at the paper.

There was general mayhem and laughter and a few people found that a task belonged in two categories. Terry encouraged them to use duplicates to move the task under both categories. One Post-It Note® for each applicable category. He shared a color marking pen and asked the team member to put an A and B on the notes for future consideration.

After the notes were all up on the paper, Terry asked for team members to go and stand with the category that interested them most. He was pleased to see that some people went to categories that were not their primary job. This gave him the mix he wanted without moving people from their voluntary position.

"Now sort through the notes and put them in order. Work as a team to determine what comes first, second, third, etc. If a task is missing, use the additional Post-It Notes® to add to the list. Run the list from left to right because we will be using the upper and lower portions to do some other things." Terry instructed.

The noise was more dynamic now and they argued over the complexities of the project. He could tell that the exchange was also educating people about the current process and that some recommendations were going to enhance the productivity.

Terry then worked them through the rest of the process, looking for tasks that needed further definition, then dependencies and finally the dots were used to find the pain and success within the process. The discussion on dependencies allowed the group to express issues about internal process as well as external deliverables not being met. Terry carefully listened and recorded these comments.

When he got the group up to display the dots for pain, slow downs, and working well he found that the group was very animated. The red dots were in three obvious spots and were creating some dialogue with various team members.

Before it became too heated, Terry stepped over and encouraged them to continue with the dot process and that he would be taking time to discuss these areas of concern.

After all the dots needed were on the butcher paper, Terry asked everyone to be seated again. "Wow, looks like we've got three major areas of *opportunity!*" The group chuckled at Terry's grin and there were a few comments like, "Yeah, right...opportunity!"

"Let's look at each one of these *hot* areas and find out what we can do about them. The only ground rule I'll set is (and he paused for effect)...this is not a blame game. This is not an opportunity to throw darts at one another. I want to hear what's happening in a factual way. AND I'd like your suggestions as to how the pain can be resolved. Is that fair?"

There were general nods of agreement but a few people looked concerned. Terry took a deep quiet breath and then said, "Some times as we work on a project, we are really great at our part and may not realize how what we do impacts others. We may not realize how long it takes for something to be done or we may not realize that the person we are waiting on is, in fact, waiting on someone else. What will help us in this discussion is to talk about what *I am experiencing*. When we stay in the *I* mode we aren't blaming others and they can express what they are experiencing without jeopardy.

"For example, I am finding that I have some very strong players on this team. They are very assertive about getting the job done. I feel challenged by this sometimes because

179

they need answers I don't have yet. This makes me feel slow and old sometimes." Terry grins at the group. There are general chuckles and a few shaking heads.

"What's important about what I just said?" Terry asked the group.

Several people offered their understanding of the process and one of his very strong players offered that maybe he needed to back off when Terry said he didn't know yet. That brought a laugh from everyone and Terry felt it was safe to move on with the exercise.

"Now if you step out of the *I* mode during your explanation all I will do is ask you to pause and consider what you are experiencing and what you would like to have instead. Then we will go to others who might have suggestions or agreements with what you said. Fair for everyone?" Terry asked and scanned the room for agreement.

Terry then pointed to the first heavily red dotted area and asked for a volunteer to share what they were experiencing in this area. Terry only had to ask for the pause twice in the discussion of all the red dot areas and many good suggestions on how to improve. One person who had obviously been seen as a target for the pain was able to express both the issues slowing the process and her suggestions for how to shift the process to allow for more effective and speedy delivery. This was well received and seemed to relieve significant stress in the room as well as develop more understanding of the process dependencies.

The final step in the day was to look at the chart again and determine what they now wanted to add (incorporate their suggestions) and then assign job titles to each task. This allowed a clear distinction of roles and responsibilities. Terry told the group that the whole chart would be typed up and distributed. He also spoke to the fact that this would be used to update the job descriptions for the group and could help them later in setting some performance goals.

He congratulated them on a successful meeting and for all their support. He asked them for some feedback on the session. What did they like best? What did they learn today that will help them in the future of the project? What would they like more of, better, or different? What questions do they feel are still open?

He then thanked them for their time and their lively support of the process. Letting them leave for the day with a feeling of success and competence was part of his goal and he felt that he had accomplished a great deal.

Terry knows that the next step is to type this chart into a document and study it for inconsistencies or for further enhancements. The last step would then be to distribute it at his next staff meeting and use it for discussions in the future as questions on process or responsibilities come to light.

Lessons Learned:

1. How else might you use this process in your business?

2. What are the most important ingredients to have a successful outcome in this methodology?

3. What did Terry do to focus discussion points throughout the session?

4. How did Terry avoid the blame game in the session?

5. What other questions would you like to add to the process to develop more effective processes?

6. Who else would you see inviting to the process development session?

7. How could you use this methodology with clients/customers? How could it be a benefit to your business?

8. What did you learn that surprised you?

9. How will that help you in your job?

10. What modifications could you make in the process for major organizational change?

Terah Stearns

Chapter 9

Communicating Change

In this communication process our focus is on change. Whenever I work with organizations going through massive change (and to some even the slightest change is massive) the most common complaint is lack of communication. When you go back and review the personality profiles we discussed in the lesson on Building High Performance Teams you will understand that some people need a lot of information to accept change or even consider it! Others will embrace change and support you through the process wholeheartedly. The key is to find a good balance as you work through the transition. This lesson is designed to help you consider that balance and develop a plan to support your staff so they can support you.

The Basics

The best way to begin is to think back to the last three changes you made in your business or organization. You can even consider your personal life. Take a moment and list all the good things you experienced as you went through the change. What worked well? Now, consider all the things you didn't like. Write these down. What did you need more of? What did you need in a different way?

Many people list a communication plan, strategy, planning, support, training, vision, and mission. Now notice I didn't say whether these items were on their good list or their bad list. These show up on both. They are necessary for any successful transition. You may have had even more on both lists. Notice them! The same things you needed are going to be needed by some or all of your organization. When any of these things are missing, people can really dig in their heels and become incredibly resistant, even *to the things they want*. In another course called Effortless Transitions, I have many support tools and an understanding of the psychology of change but for this discussion we are going to focus on the communication process.

The Intention

Many managers believe that you can just tell people what they have to do differently and people will do it. Amazing! It would be very nice if it was that simple but if you are honest you will realize it takes more to make it happen.

Consider this scenario:
I walk up to you and tell you in a nice but firm voice that I want you to stop what you are writing and begin writing with your other hand! Now unless you are one of those very rare ambidextrous people you are going to challenge this. I

tell you, "I'm sorry but I must insist that you write with your other hand because the whole department must change and change quickly."

Now how are you feeling? How do you feel about me? How do you feel about you? What would you want to do?

While this may seem a silly example it happens in many ways every day in every organization; frequently without realizing the impact it has on people.

Now imagine that I come to you and tell you that the vision and mission of the organization has changed. We need to go over here to survive. We think we want you to write with your other hand because it will get a better outcome. I list some reasons but then give it to you to decide how to get the outcome we need. What? I leave it to you to *tell me?* No, not possible!

Yes, it is. But the communication process must have defined outcomes. Remember the lesson on Expectations? When we grant people the opportunity to help us create the outcome in the way that fits them best (wherever possible) they engage fully and creatively. They come up with ideas that would have never occurred to us. As long the WHAT is fully defined allow your staff to support you in creating the HOW. You'll get better results and they'll work harder and with less resistance.

Structure and Process

The keys to success here are to define outcomes and deadlines or target dates. These are your starting points. Be very clear about each of these. When setting deadlines be sure to tell people why these dates are important, especially the benefits and/or penalties of not meeting them.

Pre-planning

It is important for upper management to be connected *and* supportive of the planned change. If they are demanding the change make sure that you have all the data.
- What are their expectations or planned outcomes?
- What dates do they expect to see met?
- How will they know you are successful?

ASK these questions. If they don't know the answers then you may want to offer your own suggestions (or recommend that you look for other ways to support their objectives once they have a real outcome.) That sounds a bit mean but all too often organizations don't think through change for the real benefits. Sometimes the benefits are smaller than the costs. Sometimes one executive wants to make an impact and your organization gets caught in the middle of the cross-fire.

So check on the real outcome and begin to form your plan. When you have clear benefits and/or penalties and dates, you can begin the transition with your team.

Explain the process of working together

It is important to understand that when you begin talking about change, people get stressed. Even people who want change will go through a mild crisis. So I like to begin with a brainstorming session. I play the "what if" game with them.

Example:
Mgr: I've been listening to the conversations at the executive level and I'm seeing some shifts. I believe they are beginning to think of adding a new product to our manufacturing line. Now we've been hitting our targets with some great results lately. When we add one or two more products to the line that means we need to be looking at efficient shifts and clear handoffs. What's important to me is to look for ways to add new products without losing our efficiencies. What's important to you?

Now the manager goes around the room gathering suggestions, which she puts on a flipchart and initial questions on another flipchart.

Points to ponder: *What's different about this process? How does it support the change process? Why would this be the second step in the communication process? What was the first step?* (Hint: clarity with your supervisor!)

Mgr: These were all good points and from the questions, I can see I have some additional information to gather. But for now we are brainstorming. This could be a major "what if" game but I like for us to stay ahead of the executives and be prepared for any contingency. It shows us to be the best team in the organization and I want to keep it that way! Agreed?

Group: You bet!

Mgr: Now looking at some of your comments, the first step is to be sure that we are working on products with mostly similar parts. Then we can easily pull the additional parts as needed with minimal change to equipment or flow. What do you see as a good mix? For instance, how much differentiation could one line handle? How much could we stockpile in additional parts without hampering the floor? What would be the fastest turn around for the line?

Hint: if you have a large group, put them into smaller groups and have them answer your questions in the separate groups and then report back. Give them each a page or a flipchart and let them brainstorm together, reporting out to the larger group. This way you get even more ideas and better synergy.

Mgr: These are great ideas. Now just out of curiosity, what do you think are the benefits to the company in doing this? *(Answers from group captured on flipchart.)* What could be the benefits to us as a team? *(Answers from group captured on flipchart. Ask each person to be sure everyone is heard.)* What are the personal benefits for you as an individual? *(Answers from group captured on flipchart. Ask each person to be sure everyone is heard.)*

Mgr: Now I'm going to ask each of you to keep these benefits in mind as we go forward. As I find out more, we'll keep brainstorming together. The good news is that we've got a jumpstart on this. Through your observations here, I can talk much more knowledgeably with the Executive Team and can make realistic suggestions as to how we could do this best. You are the experts so it pays to have you tell me what we can do. What I'd like for you to do over the next three weeks is really look at the line. Where can we improve efficiencies? What setup might make the biggest difference if we were to store 10% more parts on the floor? Is 10% the right number? What's the magic number for the amount of different products we could manufacture *efficiently?* Be prepared in next week's meeting to share some of your thoughts.

Use active learning tools

As the time rolls around for the actual change, your team has been giving suggestions and building a new process (see Developing Process Easily lesson.) Now take a session to have two teams walk through the new process with others being the evaluators. You can have some as time keepers, safety monitors and quality auditors.
- How well does the new process flow?
- Where can it be made better?
- What could you do more of, better or different?

Have your team really look at it. Have the evaluators judge the two teams and share back what they found to be successful and then have the group evaluate how to incorporate the best from both teams.

Focus the discussion

In each session take time to revisit the vision, mission and outcomes you are driving toward. Then revisit the benefits that the team said was important to them. Feel free to add to the list as they see new opportunities.

Consider Options

Your job is to keep them focused on what they *can* do. When they begin to get stuck, "take away gravity." This is a brainstorming technique to get them outside the box.

Example: "if you were in the space shuttle and parts were flying all around you what would you do to be more efficient?" "Or if you were on Jupiter and there was 100 times more gravity, what would you do to move parts more efficiently?"

At times, I give them an unlimited budget and others I give them zero budgets, more time…less time. Reshape their world so they <u>have</u> to get outside the box! Think of all the options and then pick the best. Allow the team to vote or challenge each other to test proposals and then determine the best for all. I have seen some managers have two teams with each taking the other team's proposal and doing a trial run. Then they both come back discussing what worked best in the other's design. They learn, evaluate and build off each other; developing a more comprehensive plan than if they worked as one group or as two separate teams.

Apply the information to the real world

If they are going to be asked to do something totally different from anything they have done before consider giving them a story from your past that showed how you had to overcome a new process. What you learned and how it furthered your career? Then ask each of them to share with you one of their biggest challenges. What did they learn in the end? How did they benefit from accepting the change and going forward? You are reconnecting with their ability *to change successfully.* In the stress of thinking about change, people become less resourceful and forget they change successfully all through their lives.

What to do if they get emotional

In another of my seminars, <u>Effortless Transitions,</u> I spend a great deal of time around the psychology of change and how to manage it effectively. The most important thing to remember is that they are only emotional because they are scared. Fear puts everyone in a less resourceful state. Allow them to express their fears in positive terms.

- Ask them if they have ever had to face similar fears before?
- What did they do to overcome them?
- What's different this time?
- What would they like to do differently this time?
- What support do they need (from you, from their team-mates?)

The second most important thing is not to take their emotions personally. This really isn't about you. It's plain and simple fear. If you make a big deal out of it, it will expand exponentially. If you ignore it, it will become resistance. Neither is where you need to be in the transition.

Closing

With each session, and the larger the change the more sessions you should have, take the time to consider how the employees can synthesize the information session.

Always close the session by *thanking them* for being so open to exploring more effective ways to work with their team and you. Tell them you plan to support them by noticing every instance where they bring new ideas and behaviors into the workplace. Tell them you will keep them informed when things are real but not just the rumor mill. It is important to help them see that during any proposed change there is more rumor than fact. Your job is to keep them focused on what will make the team successful. Tell them to feel free to check with you on the "rumors" but you are the source for facts!

In Conclusion

Successful, effortless change comes from clearly articulating the goal, the benefits, the plans and the deadlines. The more your team participates in the process development the more buy-in and support you will have. Resistance comes from being "done to." Buy-in comes from being "done with", which is, asked, heard and supported.

Integration Scenario:

Donna's group had always been in customer service. Their call center was one of the best in the company. The new CEO wanted to build a Quality Center (QC). Donna loved the idea and wanted to run the operation. When she spoke with the CEO he blessed the idea and told her to take her team and revamp its mission and process to support the new center.

Donna asked for six weeks to develop the process completely and transition her team. The CEO said he wanted a complete update in four weeks and then expected full implementation in six. Donna felt this was very aggressive but spent the weekend looking at the objectives of the organization. She had previously done succession planning and considered her top three people to help support the idea.

She laid out an objective overview of the new organization. She asked herself the following questions:
- What do we currently do best?
- What are we passionate about?
- What are the market indicators that drove the CEO to make this call?
- If this group was incredibly successful in setting new quality standards for the company what would that look like?
- What is the added value to the company delivered by the QC?
- What do we do or know today that is a direct compliment or process to the new QC vision?

Donna spent a lot of time on each question. She put up flipchart pages all over her office walls. Each question had its own flipchart page. As new answers came up, she wrote them down. She spent the weekend walking in and out of her home office reviewing the questions, adding, subtracting and editing her answers. By 4:00 p.m. on Sunday she had a comprehensive list and a clear vision of where she wanted to go with the group.

She typed up the draft and prepared copies for her 8:00 meeting with her "critical 3" (her future leaders.)

At 8:00 the next morning, she sat around the conference table with her critical 3 and passed out the questions and answers she had laid out for the weekend. She asked them to hold this information confidential for the next few days as she wanted to run the concept by the CEO before sharing with the staff. One of her critical 3, Jeff, asked why it needed to be held private.

Donna shared that because this was the CEO's idea, she wanted to make sure that her suggestions and vision were in alignment with his. If he had major changes, she would have gotten the staff upset for nothing. Her intention with this morning's meeting was to have the three of them do a reality check on her thoughts. She asked for their commitment to confidentiality and each nodded.

As they proceeded through the document, Donna shared her process over the weekend. She shared where she thought the team had passion and commitment toward quality and how their customer service experience could benefit this new role.

Donna asked the three to tell her where they had concerns and where she was on track. She asked for feedback in all forms and they responded with enthusiasm. Charlie had concerns about some staff that were very bonded to their special customers. He wondered whether they would be open to the change. Jeff was very concerned about the short deadline and who would take up the old process as they moved to the new one. Sharon supported the plan but wanted more time to think through it. She wanted to analyze staff skills against responsibilities. Donna made copious notes and began a spreadsheet of tactical issues to address. This would begin the transition project plan.

Donna requested that the three keep this list hidden but consider it throughout the day. They set a meeting for 4:00 that afternoon to review their additional thoughts. She told them she would type up the new ideas from this morning and put it in a neon orange folder on her desk. They were more than welcome to come by and look at it during the day if they forgot something.

After the meeting, Donna set up an appointment with the CEO for Wednesday morning. She knew her timeline was tight and she wanted to have his approval of direction sooner rather than later. It was important to have him fully committed before she brought it to her staff. She also wanted him to feel comfortable and approve the benefits and objectives she had listed since these were going to be her talking points with her staff and those organizations that she would need to work with in the future.

As Donna began to look at her communication plan it, the first draft looked like this:

Task	Outcome expected	Dept. Resp.	Comm. Method	Date/ Time req	Own
Review first draft of new mission criteria	Answer questions, Get buy-in and commitment suggestions for departments	CEO and Donna	Face to face	2 days (Wed) 1 hour	DS
Develop Mission/V ision and Values for new departmen t	Agreement on new mission, support values, look for benefits, discuss next steps and support needs	New QC group	Facilitate d session (conf. Rm. A Req)	5 days 2-3 hours	DS
Current Process review for transition planning	Review skills requirements, training of outside dept. staff, Choose interface team for supporting other dept. transition plan,	Customer Service Group (Senior Team Leads)	TBD (Conf. rm. C req.)	7 days	JB
Review process on transition	Get timelines and determine any training needs, dates for training and owners	Interface team and proposed dept. mgrs as per CEO mtg.	Facilitate d	10 days	CI
Weekly staff meeting	Updates, process planning, transition news, team reports on initiatives	Rotating with team reports, continue comm. of outcome planning and success factors	Conf. Rm. A	Every Thurs.	DS
Weekly e-news update	*Create format for this*	FAQ and updates, staff mtg. minutes	e-mail	Every Friday	ADM TML

As Donna reviewed the plan, she knew the dates and ideas would shift as the plans developed. Making the chart gave a place to start and talking points for her with staff. As the planning moved to implementation, she could also include other managers' input and staff successes in play. The critical success factor was to have consistent, honest feedback with staff and have them share in the various pieces of the process development to help them transition easier. The project plan would come next after the meeting with her critical 3 and then build off the staff facilitated meeting on Friday.

Lessons Learned:

1. What did you like best about the communication process?

2. What steps would you add?

3. What parts of the process might be challenging in your work environment?

4. What parts of the process could you use to make small changes effectively in your current organization?

5. What surprised you about this lesson?

6. What benefits would be gained by you in asking the questions Donna created to build her plan?

Terah Stearns

Chapter 10

Reporting Status

Status reports can be very effective management tools and a great way to establish communication through the chain of command. Effective status reporting can provide solutions to many of your day to day management concerns as well as human resource issues. It is important to make the reports meaningful and doable while meeting the demands of the business and using your staff's time efficiently.

The intention of status reports is to provide a means of tracking work, successes, and issues from week to week or month to month. They are useful tools for performance evaluation throughout the year. How often are performance evaluations written with only the last three months of the year in mind? Excellent work at the start of the year is forgotten or diminished by a bad project outcome at the end of the year.

Managers must hold a clear intention and remind themselves frequently that this is ultimately the way to make their job easier and have a happy, successful organization. Selling the benefits to staff on providing the reports will be a big part of this process. Initially, if no reporting structure has been in place and communication has been ad hoc or subjective, this will require some coaching and management to make it valuable. When done effectively, status reports can be powerful tools for everyone in managing up, down and sideways!

Persistence, patience, consistency, and understanding will be your cornerstones as you begin to rebuild and enhance the performance of your team. It will also be important that the status reports have a solid feedback loop so that people feel like the information is both meaningful and beneficial to them.

The Basics

What is it you want to evaluate in your organization? What does success look like? What are the issues you want to be made aware of in the process so that you can help or enhance the success of your team? These are the questions you want the status reports to reflect from staff.

How will you use these reports to continually improve your organizations performance? If they are not used to improve the operations of your organization then you may have other issues to address before instituting any kind of formal reporting structure.

Creating effective one-on-one conversations and bringing a clear communication back to the employee will make a big difference in the way they respond to the status report process.

The status reports will also provide important feedback for group meetings. When reviewing status reports, pulling out the successes of various projects and asking the employees to share their methods in a staff meeting can be a powerful way to reward and grow skills. Allowing the staff to ask questions and learn from other employees' experiences can be very helpful to the entire organization.

The Intention

Being effective in this process means getting clear on what you are attempting to do. Go back to the questions in the Basics. How enlightened are your responses to these questions? If you are using status reports only to check up on the poor performers, you will eventually diminish the performance of your power players. Consider how this process can improve your organization on all fronts.

Power players usually like to just get the job done and move on. However, they also want recognition for their work and how full their schedule is becoming. This is a great way to continuously look at work load across a team and establish where the process can improve. It will also help you with the necessary documentation and support for employees that are not performing to expectations.

Structure and Process

A solid status report will discuss several basic topics:

- Projects currently assigned
- Where are you in the project?
- Is it on time?
- What successes have you had?
- What issues may cause concern immediately or in the future?
- Where do you need support? From whom?
- What budget allocations will you require over the next month/quarter?
- Any other information that you expressed in the Basics section
- Miscellaneous (always helpful to have a block that allows for ad hoc thoughts that don't fall into the above categories.)

Introduction of process

- Let the employees know ahead of time (in a staff meeting) that these status reports are coming. Share with them your thoughts on how this will support them. What are the benefits to them? Ask them! Let them tell you what might be a benefit. You can get them started with one or two ideas of your own but let them tell you (this creates buy-in.)
- If this is a unique experience in your office (not done before or not done in a very long time,) let the employees know that you have been reviewing your management style and the organization and you know

that things need to shift to get better. Transitions and process changes are always a good lead in but do not have to be in place for this to be effective.

- Provide a template for the status report and share it with the group. Ask them what they think needs to be added. If you are willing to allow changes to the format, ask if there is any concern with any of the headings or how they might respond.

- Set an expectation that you hold this as a part of their job requirements. Reinforce the expectation by making it a formal addendum to their performance plan.

- Set a specific date to begin (if major changes do not have to be made to the template.)

- Let them know how to deliver the status report back to you or their immediate supervisor and what to expect as a result from the reporting process. *How often will you get back to them? Will this elicit a scheduled one-on-one meeting or ad hoc response?*

Note: the more effective process is to hold one-on-one meetings and use this report as the agenda, thereby allowing immediate feedback and next step generation or congratulations!

Process Starts

On or before the formal start date, deliver the agreed upon template to the staff. Have the necessary final question and answer sessions to be sure that everyone is aware of their responsibilities. Establish the time frame for reporting.

- Are you going to have them do a weekly or monthly reporting cycle? (NOTE: for different groups there can be different time frames depending on critical nature of the project or the overall performance of the group.)

- Are you going to have one-on-one meetings with them?
- Do you want the report sent to you prior to the meeting for review and analysis?

Letting the employee know what to expect helps set the stage for success by ensuring that everyone has the same basic understanding of the purpose and process.

Explain the process of working together

A brief discussion of the expectations for the employee, and the manager and what each can expect from the other helps to ground the employee in a shared sense of how to work together. Some will work from very broad guidelines and others will need very specific details. Have patience with the details and be prepared over time to coach employees as to your expectations and successful outcomes.

Understanding the types and profiles of the employee is always a nice to know and can be covered quickly with your coach/consultant.

Use active learning tools

When discussing the status report process some good questions to generate understanding and business awareness might be:

1. What do they think would be important for management to know about their projects?
2. What would help the business or clients now and in the future? (Changes to processes, policies, procedures?)
3. What stops them from being as successful as they would like? What could help them in being more effective?
4. What budget items might come up in the next quarter? Travel, entertainment, meetings, or trainings? *Note: ask them why they think this is important? This raises awareness of other parts of the business that they may not have seen as a dependency.*
5. What is it they wish they could do differently?
6. What would support them best? Who could help them?

Focus on the outcome

Remind yourself and your employees of the benefits and positive outcomes of this process and your expectations for timely delivery and effective communication. For staff that has poor writing skills or poor time management skills this will be a real stretch. However, in most cases, this raises the bar for all and gives you an effective coaching tool without having a product go out to an external organization for evaluation. It also establishes strong performance documentation for later use in the evaluation process.

Consider Options

If much of your staff is on travel or work offsite consider allowing them to send their reports via e-mail. Just be sure to have some dialogue with them on a real time basis, perhaps a scheduled conference call.

Also consider that some groups may have a very set structure to their projects. You may want to have their reports less frequently and/or have their manager/supervisor do a roll up report from their group activities. *Note: if you have performance issues in this group, you may still want to require a more structured process of reporting just to be sure that one or two poor performers are held accountable and give the power players a chance to shine. You do not want the poor performers to pull the whole group down.*

Apply the information effectively

Now how do you use all this data to run a more effective organization? Think about this carefully. Go back to your answers in the Basics. Why are you doing this?

A key success factor is having a good feedback loop. People want to know that what they are reporting is being looked at, acknowledged and used to better their jobs and their potential career aspirations. If they don't hear anything back from the work they do (no matter what you ask of them) they will eventually quit doing it. *"You obviously aren't looking so why should I bother?"*

If you work with other managers or have a management team, take the reports and consider any trends or issues that are popping up over and over again. It could be a team member that is not working effectively and may need counseling or it could be some part of the overall process that is hampering success.

The first step is to let the staff (individually) know that you have reviewed their concerns and are addressing the issues. If the process needs changing but is not in your direct control, let them know how you will be advocating for change and give them frequent updates on how you are progressing. Consider asking them if they have ideas on how they could circumvent the issue until it is fixed. Be sure it is ethical and legal and will not break any other areas of the organization!

Remember that you are also looking for successes. As you and/or your management team look for trends, notice any individual or group that consistently creates a miracle or does exceptionally good work in various areas. How can you reward this? You can make it fun or significant depending on the impact to the organization. You might consider creating a matrix of rewards that can be your guideline for performance.

Example: A review team that was called in to do a last minute travel assignment for a group that was stranded. You could have cups or caps with "SWAT Team" emblazoned on them. Can't afford that in your budget? Get a cake and have them write it in icing. The whole staff gets to enjoy but the team's names are listed and they get quick recognition for a job well done.

Example: At the end of the year, bonuses are handed out to various people. Now you have a track record of successful projects and the people that made them happen! Not only do they get rewarded but you can give explicit examples <u>and</u> re-enforce the reason it's important to write effective status reports!

What to do if the staff balks at the process

You will have some resistance as you require these reports. The first is to be sure that everyone is doing them. Be consistent. If you ask some to do them and not others, you'll have even more resistance. Remind them of the benefits (hopefully the group came up with these in your initial introduction meeting.)

When they still resist, let them know this is a job requirement. Support that you know it is extra work and you are taking this into consideration. You will be evaluating the effectiveness of the reporting process and looking for ways to help them and others do their jobs more successfully.

Be sure to have consistent feedback. The people who resist will be looking for any reason not to do the reports and no response from you says "nobody's looking!"

Summary

Status reporting can be a highly effective tool to manage staff and create positive results for your business or organization. Reporting alone will not create a miracle.

Making sure that you analyze what you are seeing, creating effective feedback loops with staff and rewarding success will lead to an organization that continuously improves and self-corrects. Establish a plan for implementation, offer a format to use for discussion and create a timely delivery mechanism. Then be sure you are doing your part to monitor, evaluate, correct, counsel and support your staff. It's a winning combination.

A sample status report:

To:	Supervisor's name
From:	Employee's name
Reporting Dates:	Month of October, 20xx or Week of October 11, 20xx

Project Status

*List all projects that are currently assigned to you. Only update specific projects being met or worked with this reporting period. If a project is on hold or having specific issues that are relayed in other sections, please highlight with color or **bold** font.*

Project Name	Date Visited	Outcome	Project Status
XYZ Corp	10/17/xx	Met with Exec. Director and Board for initial findings	Will require TA support and PCER for more specific improvements. Believe the overall organization may be having financial difficulties due to...

Successes!

Where have you been successful or created an outcome that you would like to record for your manager's awareness?

During my visit to XYZ corp. I identified a specific issue ... and was able to resolve it within 15 minutes. This led to...

Terah Stearns

Issues or Concerns

What would you like for your manager to be aware of and/or follow up with you before the next reporting cycle?

> I am concerned with the current…and would like assistance in the following manner…

Budget

Please list any budgetary items that may need to be reviewed or approved over the next 3 months. This may include but is not limited to: travel, training …

Budget item	Date required	Amount requested (if known)

Kudos for team members

If there is someone you would like for management to recognize or be aware of their special activities, please let us know here.

Name	Description of special activities	How it supported you or the team

Other Items/Miscellaneous

Please feel free to offer suggestions or comments that do not fit under other categories already listed.

Lessons Learned:

1. How might this be helpful for you in managing your staff?

2. What items would you expect to see in a status report for your staff?

3. What parts of the sample status report would work for your team?

4. What methods of delivery would work best for you and your staff?

5. What would encourage your staff to create status reports?

6. How would the status report be a benefit to your staff?

Chapter 11

Rewarding and Acknowledging

Performance

Many managers tend to over reward and/or under recognize, both of which can be detrimental to a positive work experience for the employee. The struggle is always to set meaningful expectations and objective ways of determining good performance. In some positions this is an easy task as the metrics are easily reported. But in most jobs and most companies this isn't an easy accomplishment. In the prior lessons we have discussed ways to get employee input. This is a great place to get their help. Asking how they would like to be recognized and by what measurements can be effective in building confidence and *esprit de corps*.

The Basics

Money is frequently the primary reward mechanism in business. The fact is that in surveys, money is not at the top of the acknowledgements and rewards that employees demand. It is usually about half way down the list and in some cases at the bottom. Money is usually strongly diluted by taxes and deductions and the rush only lasts for a moment. Making rewards and recognition a part of your business culture and supported by everyone is critical to the continuous success of your team. In this chapter we'll explore how to make this easy, fun and within any budget.

The Intention

The intention is to recognize excellence and support the desired behaviors in your organization. Make it easy and thoughtful for everyone to be acknowledged and to be able to recognize their team mates. This helps build confidence and spirit in any organization. Everyone excels at something. The more we acknowledge this excellence the more of this excellence we will see. Even small improvements observed and commented upon will generate great results as confidence builds from the recognition.

Structure

The first step is to determine what behaviors and values are important to you and the success of your team. Create a list and ask for input from your team. Use one of your sessions discussed earlier (or several of the various venues) to gather ideas. Look at this list and prioritize it. You may find that the criteria are so interrelated that you cannot choose one above another. This prioritization is important to help evaluate levels of awareness so take time to review. Particularly look at what *isn't* happening that needs to be present in your organization.

Also look for conflicting behaviors and messages. For example: Are there places where you want good customer service AND fast delivery? Sometimes these cause real conflict and ultimately dissension as people receive these mixed messages from management. In your review process a discussion with your team can be highly effective. (We'll explore this more in a later example.) This doesn't mean that fast delivery and good customer service can't go together. It does mean that one can be an excuse for the other not happening.

A good way to proceed from here is to set values next to each item. Use a scoring system from 1-10 or 1-100 to set importance. This will help you think through what's most important and what needs to have focus.

When the list is made and prioritized (scored) then consider how often you expect this to happen. Make another column on your list and mark it for frequency. You may use "D" for daily, "W" for weekly, etc. or you may choose to use "C" for constantly, "O" for occasionally, etc. Choose what works best for you.

I love to use a software spreadsheet for this so that I can quickly sort the categories. This allows me to see what is important and why. It also helps me to see whether my thought process is logical. If a category has risen to the top of the list because I gave it a high score and frequency but it really isn't that important in the larger context, I can quickly adjust the scoring. (Something that is not so easy on paper!)

Now that you have the list, look for ways to measure the categories. Are there metrics to show how often they are done? Will these show quality and quantity? Is that important for this category? We are looking for subjectivity *and* objectivity.

Some categories that you choose will only be evaluated by customers or colleagues. How will you determine this? Can you do an instant survey for all customer contacts? Can you do 360-degree reviews or is it more appropriate to allow employees to recognize each other?

Consider Options

As mentioned earlier, there are times when conflicts in the nature of excellence can occur. Taking these inconsistencies to your staff can create some great outcomes. Give them an opportunity to address where they see issues that may cause differences. Be clear about the ultimate outcomes you need. You can set a soft-sided box within which they need to work.

For instance: *We need to take as many calls as possible in the timeliest fashion. The way we have measured this is with the metric calls per hour per person. We look for 10 calls per hour per person. This means that on average we should be talking to the customer for six minutes. (One side of the box.)*

We also need to create a good customer experience. (The other side of the box.)

1. *What can we do to meet both of these?*
2. *What would you do if you were managing the call center?*

3. *What would you expect if you were our customer?*
4. *What would support this?*

Asking these questions can lead to extremely positive outcomes.

Here is a working example from one of my customer engagements:

Manager: "While reviewing our goals, I noticed a possibility for conflicting intentions. I measure time on call and time to resolution. I also measure the customer satisfaction in a separate survey. I realize this could be a mixed message. What is your experience?"

Allowing the team to discuss this gave a powerful opportunity to re-set expectations, to establish which was more important and had the team assist in developing new processes supporting both.

NOTE: This particular example is a fairly typical example in a call center environment when you are measuring number of calls handled and time to resolution. While the employee can resolve the problem with a quick answer there are times when customer satisfaction suffers if the customer feels unheard, rushed or doesn't know how to implement the fix suggested.

This innovative team created a separate group (only 3 people) to handle transferred calls for in-depth support. They also later developed a clever FAQ (Frequently Asked Questions) that helped users which could be faxed or e-

mailed to the client. If the client had further questions, they could call back into the center.

RESULTS: Customer satisfaction went up significantly (almost 50%) with this small introduction of support. They rotated staff through this small group so that everyone had relief from the day to day calls and had a lot of fun building the FAQ document. They added cartoon drawings and put fun customer comments in the bottom of the document to further their morale and engage the customer.

They saw these activities as their solution and morale went up significantly. They developed amusing ideas to reward the biggest contributors to the FAQ document and had an entertaining corkboard set up in the call center for the funniest question of the day. Some of these were customer questions that were truly hilarious and others were the silliest mistake an employee had made. People loved reading the day's contributions during their breaks and the comments were always lively during team meetings. Later they came up with the "rubber chicken" award for the goofiest mistake of the week. The rubber chicken was posted on the outside of their cubicle and was frequently seen wearing hats, glasses, gloves and shoes of dubious origins.

By asking one question, the manager was able to solve many problems. Customer satisfaction went up, the staff morale increased and a new solution oriented product was developed. When the manager asked the question to resolve conflict and allowed the staff to brainstorm better methods, great results ensued. Best of all, the only expense was a $4.98 rubber chicken. It's not about money! It's about *respect, recognition and realization of the employee's ideas.*

Respect, Recognition and Realization

After analyzing hundreds of employee surveys the critical message is always respect, recognition and realization (follow-through.) Real rewards and recognition come down to the following:

1. *Do you hear me?*

2. *Do you respect what I am saying?*

3. *Do you know that I care and want to make this a better place to work?*

4. *How will you allow me to participate in making this a better place to work?*

5. *How will you support me in implementing my suggestions?*

If these questions cause some concern for you, realize that many companies react the same way. That's why they fail to do any follow-up on surveys to effectively shift the culture. How often have you participated in a survey and never received any feedback on concerns or outcomes from the survey? How likely were you to participate the next time you were asked for response?

As you read through the five questions above and felt some tension (if any) it is more important to realize where your concern originates and how to handle it more resourcefully. What are you attached to? What do you really want? What stops you from getting it? There are many ways that a coach or consultant might help you quickly work through this. Ask a mentor or someone you truly respect to ask you these questions. Answer honestly and look at what you are experiencing. Ask your mentor how they would answer the five questions above. You may see a significant difference. Truly powerful, effective leaders will say YES to the first three questions and have powerful answers to support #4 and #5.

Allow yourself to play with these questions and ask yourself: If I knew that letting my employees support the process and implement their own suggestions would bring me untold success, what would I do differently? How would I respond to these questions if I realized the power of their ideas and motivation?

You know what happens when you ignore and reject employee's ideas. Turn it around and see the power working for you! This is without a doubt the greatest way to recognize and reward your staff. Being allowed to fully participate in the success of the organization is a powerful gift. It shows you respect them and appreciate them. You will stand out among management as an enlightened leader and you will get better results every time because your staff will own the outcomes.

In Conclusion:

Make your list and prioritize for behaviors that are worth recognizing and rewarding. Check with your staff for their suggestions and recommendations. Allow them to check for inconsistencies or goals that might conflict. Ask them for ways to create new behaviors and ways to reward and recognize them. Challenge them to have fun with their ideas. Then be sure to follow through. Give your staff updates on progress for any rewards that require time to process or if you are still looking for the "rubber chicken!" Most of all realize that great leadership is all about recognizing the strengths and positive behaviors and abilities in your organization. It does not always require money to make people happy. It does take your time and commitment!

Integration Scenario:

Kevin walked into the organization knowing that there were problems. You couldn't miss them in the team interviews. He knew that the previous manager had sent very conflicting messages to staff and that morale was as low as productivity. No surprise there! What he did want was a quick turn around for the department.

Kevin set down one night and began to think about what success would look like for the department. What would it feel like? What would it sound like? He future paced and saw himself three months ahead walking through the department. What did he see? What did he hear?

Then Kevin began to make a list of the behaviors he could see in his vision. He listed things that he wanted customers to say to him about people. He listed things that he wanted to see from staff in general. He began to get excited.

After he made the list, he began to prioritize. He shifted many things around and finally determined that there were six things he most wanted to see over the next three months. He knew that some of them would appear to be conflicting for employees and would require discussion. He put this list on the agenda for Monday's staff meeting.

On Monday morning, Kevin passed out the list of "successful behaviors." When the meeting began he asked staff if these behaviors would be of value to them. He asked what each would look like if they were a consistent part of the organization. He allowed the discussion to run freely and captured some notes on the white board.

"What would be the benefit to us as a department if we exhibited these behaviors constantly?" He asked.

Some positive comments came from the group but he saw that one or two were sitting back from the conversation.

"Do you see any of these behaviors as contradicting each other or any other objectives of the company?" He inquired.

"Yeah," Eric said, "I think fast delivery may get in the way of quality service."

"Tell me more." Kevin requested.

"If we want to be sure that the product arrives safely then getting it out the door fast doesn't fit." Eric said.

"I can see where that might happen. Is there anyway to do both?" Kevin prompted.

"I think we *can* do both but we need to look at our packing process to make some improvements and streamline some things." Shawna volunteered.

"Great! What would you suggest?" Kevin asked.

The conversation continues and then Kevin posed the next question, "What could we do to recognize when people on the team are really doing a great job of meeting these objectives? When we see people doing a quality job and getting it done fast, how could we recognize and/or reward them?"

"More money" was a quick response but others recommended mentioning it in the staff meeting and creating a "wall of fame" with quick photo shots of the people. Others recommended a special card that they could give to team members that helped make things happen. The cards could be turned in for prizes or a free day off! The excitement generated from this discussion spoke of a positive morale building in the team.

Kevin asked for how to measure the success of the new behaviors so that the whole department could see the benefits in living to them. There were some metrics already in place, like order to ship, returns for damages, etc.

Kevin then asked, "So what should the numbers be on these?" Kevin knew what management said they should be but he wanted his people to set the first target.

On some of the numbers the team was more aggressive than management's numbers. On other metrics they set a lower target because they were so far away from the company's targets. Kevin then asked them how soon they'd like to start hitting their objectives. Again some were immediate and some were way out on the calendar. Kevin asked them to pick a target date within the quarter and if they needed to set an interim metric, he was okay with that also.

Kevin noted that some of the employees were surprised at his open demeanor. But as a group they committed to metrics and dates. Then he asked what they should do to celebrate when they hit the target. Again, he noted surprise but the energy in the room went to a new high. They decided on a cookout in the park near their building and a long lunch. He agreed.

He told them that he was going to take all their suggestions and work on the "instant recognition" system they had discussed with the cards and the wall of fame. He promised to have a clear plan by their next staff meeting.

He then thanked them for their time and support and reassured them that he felt that he'd be cooking hamburgers next month! They laughed and started to disperse.

Several of his staff stopped to thank him for the session and many said they thought this would be fun! Kevin smiled as he gathered his notes from the meeting. They had some good suggestions and he felt he could easily build on them. It was time to start implementing the recognition plan and he felt he had commitment from the group. The key was follow up and execution.

He would create a permanent space on the meeting agenda for recognition and promote each improvement in the numbers by asking what worked and how it benefited the team. Then he'd challenge them to take it to the next level.

They were on their way to surprising management with their new attitude and intention.

NOTE: Over the last 25 years, I have had this same meeting with every organization I have been asked to support. I have found that results happen very fast and the energy of the group builds on each new success as long as I make a focus of the success. Sometimes even small successes create the biggest impact; especially in the early stages. In one instance, the earlier example of the call center, we marked a significant improvement in less than 30 days. By the end of the quarter, the manager had the pleasure of reporting the best metrics and customer satisfaction rating in the company's history. He shared the success openly with his staff every week.

By the end of the fiscal year, they were outpacing every department in the company for efficiency and customer satisfaction. They had cut the budget by 20% and not had a single layoff. Morale was higher than ever and where many call centers have as much as 50% turnover, they were in the single digit turnover rates. This reduced training requirements and increased the knowledge base for easier customer support, shorter time to resolution of problems.

One of the biggest hidden opportunities was with the increase in efficiency they began to establish ways to improve the products. They developed a system to capture and report problems so that the programmers and technicians could FIX problems so they disappeared off the radar. This again, reduced calls, increased efficiency, lowered budgets and increased morale. All of this because he set the system in place to listen, recognize and reward his people for the objectives and behaviors that support success. People respond to recognition of their accomplishments!

Lessons Learned:

1. What's the first step in setting a reward and recognition process for your organization?

2. What is already in place that can be expanded to include more people and quicker recognition?

3. How would this process benefit you?

4. What key metrics might be valuable in recognizing?

5. In making your list of behaviors and objectives, how many can you think of immediately? Which are most important?

6. If you were to benchmark morale in your organization, using a one-ten rating (10 highest morale,) how high would you set the current benchmark?

7. How high could it be at the end of the next quarter if you were to implement the process tomorrow?

8. What would be the benefit to your staff?

9. Using examples from the lesson, what could this process do *for the business or organization that would be meaningful?*

10. What would stop you from implementing this process?

11. What can you do to make the process happen? (How can you overcome any roadblocks or create new ways to make the recognition process happen in your organization?)

Chapter 12

Appraising Performance

Do you feel a shudder at the dreaded words *performance appraisals (PA)?* Many managers feel the same way. Whether you do PA on a quarterly, semi-annual or annual basis, the task can be daunting. If you do them quarterly, they come far too often. If you have a large number of direct reports you can spend your life doing appraisals and nothing else. If you do them on a semi-annual or annual basis, they seem so far apart as to be ineffective. How do you remember what was done in the early part of the year? How do you have a meaningful conversation when you are covering that span of time?

Does all of this sound too familiar? Are you hoping this can be easily resolved?

Using the process described here and in the chapters suggested below, you will find Performance Appraisals much easier, less time consuming and *even* pleasurable. *Yes, pleasurable!* You'll find you have better results, happier employees and lower blood pressure.

Terah Stearns

The Basics

Effective Performance Appraisals (PA) provides a support process for leadership to communicate expectations and vision to the organization. They provide the opportunity to learn together and to work on the issues needing to be addressed. In addition to encouraging the exchange of information and creating learning experiences, managers assist direct reports in sorting through difficult choices and discussing the implications and decisions that arise from developing deeper levels of understanding. Effective managers provide a neutral and factual context for their direct reports, guide and maintain the process, and work with their employees to figure out how to help them achieve their objectives.

Intention

Performance appraisals are an opportunity for the employee to share their successes, ask for support and discuss their challenges. Viewing PA as a positive exchange and a chance to catch potential issues early by relaying your expectations clears the way for success. Setting a process that supports this dialogue and maximum input from the employee makes it enjoyable for you and the employee.

Session Structure and Process

Various Performance Appraisal processes drive the exact structure used, however many sessions follow a basic formula that can be customized based on the employee and the issues to be discussed.

Pre-session Planning

- To the extent possible, involve participants in the performance appraisal. Get ideas before the appraisal

236

meeting and check in with the employee at the start of the meeting to see if anything is missing. I used to do quarterlies. When one was due, I would send out a copy of the last one to the employee in a "personal and confidential" envelope asking them to review it, make any notes and send it back to me prior to the meeting. I consistently had among the highest scores in my peer group for the 'trust and confidence in my immediate manager' category (employee surveys.)

- Imagine several scenarios for how the conversation might play out, and how you will respond.
- Make a "talking points" memo to refer to specific issues that need to be addressed so that you are not lost in the appraisal form.
- Consider effective questions to be asked that will support your conversation and awaken the employee to more awareness of the business and his/her contribution. *(See lesson on Communicating Effectively.)*

Session Opening

Provide some common context for the employee by answering these questions: What is the importance of the performance appraisal? What are the key topics to be addressed? Tell them how you wish to conduct the session. Letting the employee know what to expect helps set the stage for a successful discussion by ensuring that everyone has the same basic understanding of the purpose and agenda.

Rules and Tools: Explain the process of working together

A brief discussion of the expectations for the employee, the manager and what each can expect

from one another helps to ground the employee in a shared sense of how to work together. Some employees use formal ground rules; others set broad expectations and address more specific issues later in the meeting, as needed.

Set the stage for the appraisal. Let the employee know that you consider this an open dialogue and have reviewed the objectives set in the previous review as well as their comments on the current period. Let them know that you are looking for their successes and challenges to develop a training or support plan for their continuous improvement.

Rules and Tools: Use active learning tools

Experiential activities, such as opportunities to practice applying concepts, interaction with manager on specific topics, hands-on demonstrations, role plays, etc. all stimulate the employee to participate actively, rather than listening passively to the appraisal.

As the discussion unfolds look for ways for the employee to see their job in relationship to the overall business objectives. Ask them how they fit in and how their role is important to the success of the organization and their team members. Build their awareness for future performance objectives and critical thinking skills.

Focus the discussion

Narrow the focus of the conversation to a topic that can realistically be covered in the time available. Break down performance to specific topics and deal with critical items only. Ask the employee to express what s/he believes *success* would look like in these performance issues. It is very easy to get into a *laundry list* of critical points. PA is the time to create a focused solution to effective participation in the company.

Example: You have an employee who frequently comes in late, misses deadlines and is late for many meetings. The real topic is time management and requirements of the job. If not addressed you may find yourself with a much bigger problem requiring a performance improvement plan and possible termination.

Begin by saying: "What's important to me is for you to become more consistent in your performance. I need you to manage your time more effectively. This will increase your career opportunities and provide me with an idea of your skills and abilities rather than focusing on what is not happening."

- *Question to employee: "What's important to you?"*
- *Listen carefully to seek understanding.*
- *Ask "what stops you from meeting deadlines and being on time?"*
- *Again, listen for what stops them or is creating such poor performance.*
- *Question to employee: "What would success look like if you were able to manage your time more effectively?"*
- *Listen carefully. Look for their awareness of success and whether they are seeing the bigger picture. Do 'they really know what you expect?*
- *For more effective questioning techniques see lesson on "Communicating Effectively."*

Example: If the employee is not making the connection in regards to their time management performance, ask them if they have ever been in a meeting or session where the critical people did not arrive on time and caused others to wait?

How did that make them feel? What's important to notice about this? How does it relate to what they are doing to others in the organization? What important information do they miss when they are late? What other deadlines or business activities do they affect when they turn work in late?

As you can see these questions put the responsibility back on them to determine the effects of their behaviors. If they are not able to make the connection then directive conversation will be required. But understand that *"telling"* has little or no impact on people. The true changes come from their decisions about their behaviors. The more you create a *learning process* for them the faster they will change their behavior.

Rules and Tools: Apply the information to the real world

> Consider using a case study or testing the decisions on an actual issue brought forward by the employee to help him/her understand how to put into practice the knowledge they have gained.

Ask them to give you a scenario. "Tomorrow morning, what will you do differently to manage your time more effectively?"

After the two of you have spent time discussing various scenarios, *future pace* them. Ask them to see one year (quarter or 6 months, depending on PA requirements) from now. What will this conversation look like for the two of you when the employee is now practicing all the new behaviors they have developed in your meeting today? Allow them to really turn up the volume on this. Now ask them how this will affect their career. This will allow them to *lock in* the benefits of these new behaviors.

Closing

Consider how the employee can synthesize the information session. Bring closure to the session by asking for feedback, drawing conclusions, identifying next steps, or simply sharing information about the experience of learning.

Ask them for signatures on the forms, if required. If they require time to review what was written, allow them to read through the report and ask them if they understand how what was written supports the conversations and ideas that they offered during the session. (If you have time, it is always very effective to write the form together.)

Close as usual with appreciation for their openness and commitment to change.

In Conclusion

Notice how little the manager needed to do in this process. Your primary function was to develop the key *talking points* and

then ask *effective questions* to draw out the awareness of the employee.
Now:

- Make copies of the signed appraisal
- Turn in a copy to HR (or Personnel)
- Give the employee a signed copy (with a little sticky note attached saying, "thanks for a good session.")
- File your copy.
- AND BREATHE a sigh of relief (for a job well-done!)

Integration Scenario:

Kim faced the calendar and sighed. The semi-annual performance reviews were due in six weeks. With 14 people reporting to her that was a sizable task in a relatively short time.

Kim had a process though that worked well and seemed to assure her staff. She began to pull employee files, seven at a time. She pulled the old performance appraisal (PA) out of the file and put a sticky note hanging out of the file. When she had the first seven, she went to the copier and made two copies. Putting one of each in a separate folder, she went back to her office and put the originals back in their folder and did the remaining seven. She found this helped her since interruptions could cause her to become distracted and lose files or originals.

After making all the copies, she marked one folder "for my review and action." The other folder, she marked "to employees." She pulled a stack of confidential internal office envelopes and put them with the second folder. During quiet moments she created a confidential envelope with a personal note to the employee attached to the old copy of their PA. Her note asked for their thoughts on their significant achievements, development/training accomplishments, and development issues for the future. She asked for the return of the PA within two weeks, detailing the date in the note.

Each envelope was delivered during the next day and Kim began to prepare for her work on the new appraisals. Each morning she pulled an employee folder and read through her notes for the last 6 months, making her comments on the old PA as to success or still needs development or training. She also noted changes to their current assignments and issues that needed counseling.

As employees returned their PA with their comments, it was easy for her to take her notes and theirs to create the new PA. By the end of the third week, she was ready to start meeting with each employee. She sent meeting notices to each and asked them to mark the time on their calendars. She set aside one hour for each and had three weeks to complete the meetings. She found that on average it took 30 to 45 minutes for each session.

She built a short list of talking points for general discussion, especially targeted on the new goals and objectives of the business. She used this to raise awareness and help develop a powerful discussion on performance enhancements. She had found that talking about what was important to the business and the group, kept the performance issues focused and set benefits for the change. It also kept the dialogue from becoming emotional if the issue was a mismatch of goals rather than a lack of desire or commitment. When the discussion did become emotional, it was easier to redirect it to what could be done rather than "what's wrong with me, the company, or the group."

Each day, Kim felt a sense of satisfaction. She found that the employees felt good about being able to express their accomplishments and to have a specific conversation about the goals of the company and how their job directly impacted success.

One conversation that Kim had not looked forward to having was with George. During the last review, George had been meeting expectations and marginal on productivity goals. During the last six months, Kim had counseled him on two different occasions. The first discussion had been about attitude toward customers that had resulted from two fairly stringent letters from customers. George had corrected the situation and had even reconnected with the customers in a very positive way. When Kim had done a follow-up call with both customers a month later, they were satisfied that George was working well with them and no further action was necessary.

The second counseling session had been two months later when George had erupted during a staff meeting and caused considerable hurt feelings in the team. While he had apologized to the group after the counseling there were still moments of tension when his comments bordered on rude. Kim had taken action by commending him when she saw better interaction with co-workers and worked with him on reasons for the stress. His productivity was still marginal and he was going to receive a "meets expectations" for the second time in a row. This effectively meant a cost of living raise and Kim felt sure that this could be received with anger. Preparing her talking points for the conversation, Kim focused on what he had achieved and where she had seen improvements. What was important for her to find out was George's commitment level to improving.

After a brief welcome and compliment on some of George's accomplishments for the year, Kim took George through the rest of the PA documentation.

Kim: George, there have been some rough spots over the last six months I was very pleased with the way you resolved the customer service issues. When I did the follow-up call with both clients, they were content to work with you and felt that the issues were resolved to their satisfaction. Certainly, I would have preferred not to have had either incident but I was proud of you for stepping up to the plate and making them happy with us again.

As I mentioned in the earlier part of our discussion, two of the companies objectives are to improve customer satisfaction and sell deeper into their organizations. We can't meet that goal if we don't have happy customers. Thank you for resolving these situations.

George: I'm glad it got resolved. I didn't think it should have been that big a deal in the first place.

Terah Stearns

This comment raised concerns for Kim but she continued with the conversation to see what else might ensue.

Kim: Any time a client is unhappy, it can be a very big deal. It is hard for us to have a good day everyday and that's why the team created the buddy system to support the clients. Have you used it to support your customers since the two situations?

George: No, I don't like to hand off my work to Chris.

Kim: Tell me about that?

George: We're both busy and it takes too much explanation to hand them off.

Kim: I can understand you feel that way. Does Chris ever hand off work to you?

George: Yeah, quite often.

Kim: What stops you from doing the same with him?

George: I don't know. I just don't like to hand things off. I think I should do my own work.

Kim: That's a powerful principle. It shows accountability. I went through a lot of that when I first became a manager. Do you remember how I was two years ago?

George: No, not really.

Kim (smiling): It was a long time ago in the business world but I seem to remember you were one of the ones that told me to back off a little and let you take care of some stuff. I was not delegating at all and had a tendency to micromanage everything.

George: Oh yeah, I do remember. But you really let go and started giving us more of a voice in what we wanted to do and that's when we started creating things like the buddy system.

Kim: That's right. You and other team members really helped me see that I could not do it alone. It took me a while to let go. I was raised to do my own work and be accountable. I was responsible for the job and the outcome. But I've found that the power of working together as a team has been a joy. I couldn't have come up with all the processes and improvements we now have alone.

I know that I would be so stressed all the time that I'd be barking orders and driving you all nuts with my micromanaging.

George (smiled): Yeah, you sort of started out that way. You had been a great team player and then you really changed when they made you a manager.

Kim: I think I was afraid I'd fail. I was afraid I'd be a terrible manager and that the company would think they had made the wrong decision. Funny thing though, because of my fear, I was actually creating the very thing I was afraid of...

George: Yeah, we all were beginning to wonder about you.

Kim: And...you had the courage and foresight to let me know that you needed something else from me. You gave me a chance to see your side and your needs. I appreciate that a lot. It was an important turning point for me. We can't do any of this alone. We are a team. There's a lot less stress when we share the load and still maintain our accountability. We agreed that the buddy system would support us in good times and bad. Do you remember some of the benefits we determined?

George: Yeah, the main one was that when we were really stressed we would take the paperwork load and the other would have the customers. We felt this would improve our customer service and make our jobs more fun and collaborative.

Kim: Do you think it can still work?

George: Yes, I do. I realized while you were talking that I was afraid too. I didn't want Chris to think I wasn't doing my job or that he might find something in my notes that was wrong.

Kim: George, if you checked my stuff, you'd find mistakes. I am not perfect. I do an extremely good job but I'm not perfect and I'd bet you've found mistakes in Chris's work, too.

George: A few. Not many. He's really good.

Kim: George, what's important to me is not perfection. The things important to me are a good, solid, <u>happy team,</u> great customer service, and making this company successful. It takes all of us to that. Now what's most important to you?

George: I'd like to feel good about my job...you know, successful.

Kim: What does success look like, George?

George: Well, I'd like to come to one of these meetings without feeling like I was in trouble. I'd like to get a good raise and a promotion. I'd really like to have your job one day.

Kim: What do you think it takes to have all of those things happen for you?

George: Well, I gotta' stay out of trouble first. (He gave a knowing grin with this statement.)

Kim: Good one, what else? (Kim smiled.)

George: I think I've got to share the load and really work with Chris and the others. I've got to see that it's not about me but about the team and the company. I've got to stop worrying about being perfect or better than others and start being a good team member.

Kim: What can I do to support you in this?

George: Well…(he thought for a few seconds.) These conversations help. I appreciate that you don't lecture. I know what you are telling me and I see how it would help. I'm not sure what you can do other than kick me in the rear every now and then. I think I'd like to think about it for awhile.

Kim: I'm fine letting you think about it. I'd prefer not to have to kick you though. What about a pat on the back for things that are working for you? What about including a section on your status report that says "where I shared this week?" That would call it to your attention at least once each week and make it a focus rather than an after thought. How would that work for you?

George: We could try it. It might work. Knowing that I have to report something would encourage the behavior. I hate to leave anything "due" blank.

Kim (smiling): Good, let's try that then. Anything else you think of is game too, okay?

George: Yeah. I think I'll talk with Chris about this too. Maybe he can be the one to push me to do the buddy system. He can sure see when I'm stressed since we sit right across from each other.

Kim: That might be a good idea for both of you. Of course, the real responsibility lies with you. Chris may not be aware of what stresses you, right?

George: Yeah. I won't put it all on him.

Kim: Good. Now, let's look at what needs to happen between now and the next appraisal period so you get more of the success you want...

Kim knew she would observe George closely in the next few weeks so she could reinforce any positive outcomes and suggest new behaviors. She felt that he had a better grasp of what was expected and she hoped that no further action would be needed. She chose not to dwell on the smaller issues as she felt sure that they were really just spilling over from his lack of delegation skills. She would just keep an eye on the situation and hopefully next year she'd see a bigger difference and be able to reward him for great work.

While George had hoped for more pay increase, he expressed that he was pleased that she still gave him credit for his work. He knew he could do better in the future. They both agreed it was a team effort.

Lessons Learned:

1. What new ideas were stimulated by this lesson?

2. What areas of the PA are challenging for you?

3. What does a successful PA look like for you?

4. What areas of the PA would you most like to improve?

5. What tracking mechanisms do you use to evaluate performance on a regular basis?

6. What is the importance of dealing with performance issues in a timely fashion for the PA process?

Chapter 13

Improving Performance

The performance improvement process (PIP) is seldom easy from an emotional standpoint and my intention here is to help you create a less threatening and more supportive way to handle this process. We'll look at the PIP from a broader view than just the actual one-on-one PIP delivery and create a mindset that will support all your management activities so that when the time comes for the one-on-one you and your employee can be assured of an easier, painless process.

The Basics

The PIP is a much larger process than the actual document. If you are an empowering leader, you set the stage for all performance objectives during the orientation of an employee – day one. If your employee is honestly surprised by the PIP, you missed some golden opportunities to avoid this situation. Let that soak in for a moment.

If your employee is *honestly surprised* by the PIP or anything in the document *you* missed numerous golden opportunities throughout the performance period for learning, development, and better productivity from this individual. That's a tough statement and very true. We dread the PIP because we know we probably missed having the really critical conversations and now we (and the employee) have our backs to the wall.

Take a moment and think back on all the other lessons you have read here and review how many of them gave you an opportunity to set expectations, build critical awareness of the business and the results needed for top performance and the opportunity for balanced feedback throughout the year with the employee.

The opportunities clearly exist in:
- Setting Expectations
- Gaining Buy-in
- Coaching
- Process Development
- Vision, Mission and Values
- Effective Status Reporting
- Powerful Performance Appraisals

Each of these provides a unique and powerful opportunity to create clarity around the expected outcomes and develop your people to maximum performance.

When you have done all of this and he or she still is not performing, then you know, at all levels, intellectually and emotionally, they are not the right person for this job. And the important part to this is they will know it too.

The Intention

Throughout this book we have held the intention that people are inherently good, capable and willing to perform at their highest and best if we as leaders support them, effectively communicate with them, and create a process to help them be successful. When the time comes to address performance issues, we have an obligation to be direct; make it clear that they need to choose wisely and they have a short space of time to make the change. When you go in for surgery, you want the doctor to use the sharpest scalpel he has and make a clean, precise cut in the most effective way. Do it once, do it right and help them leave or improve with dignity.

Structure and Process

In so many coaching sessions with clients, they are having trouble making the decision to fire someone even though they need to make some management decision on the person. They are clear that allowing the person to continue their current behaviors is detrimental to the organization. The manager is clear that the staff's morale is affected by this poor performer. The manager also is concerned with how to do the PIP and in all honesty, they worry whether they have done their job well enough to make the PIP stick.

The Structure

Things that you must consider prior to the PIP:

- Did you set clear expectations?
- Did the employee truly know what successful performance looked like?
- In their heart of hearts, do they know this is coming?

The PIP process is a four step process that can stop at any step that successfully produces improvement. This section will provide an overview of the four steps and then I will go into more detail.

- Step one: A verbal warning.
- Step two: A 'review of outcomes' meeting with documentation as to the results of improvement or lack thereof.
- Step three: The PIP document setting a limited time frame with clear performance objectives.
- Step four: Full termination.

In step one, the verbal warning, you once again review expectations and gain clarity as to what top performance looks like, how you will measure it and the timeframe you are allowing to see the change. This can be as little as two weeks and as much as one month. Never drag this on for too long. Time is of the essence when you come to this decision. We will go over this in more detail but I highly recommend that you make personal documentation of this conversation. It could be useful later in future conversations.

Step two will be documented with the employee. In this conversation, you will be pointing back to the verbal warning and what is not happening. You will share with them that you will be documenting this discussion and that it will go into their permanent file.

Step three is a formal PIP. I recommend that you engage Human Resources (HR) or Personnel for this part of the process. Although I have a suggested format for the document your organization, I'm sure has their own legally approved format and you want to be very careful to follow their guidelines. I usually ask for an HR representative to be present for these meetings as well. First as a witness for the documentation *and* as an objective observer in case some miscommunication occurs. You will want to prep HR as to the issues as well as what you hope to accomplish during the session.

Step four is full termination. This may be handled completely by HR but more than likely they will ask you to play some role in the process. You may need to be present when they make the termination effective. You may also be asked to play the role of escort to help the employee pack their desk. Whenever possible, have their desk packed up for them being careful to do this respectfully and quietly. The best rule is "if this were me what would I hope would be done for me?" No matter how bad their performance or behavior, they are still human beings and they are scared. Humiliating them in the process serves no one. Hold the intention in process and languaging that termination is because the *job* did not fit the skills, interests and values of the person, not the other way around. Ninety-nine percent of the time, we made mistakes in the *hiring process*. Both of us, the manager and the employee are now correcting the mistake. If we keep the termination out of the context that the "person is wrong or bad," we all leaving whole and human; our spirits and values intact. Always remember that when we fire badly we damage our reputation and the company's.

The Process – Step One

It will be helpful to review "Setting Expectations" for a general feel for the questions and process. However, the tone of this meeting is much more directive. You want to maintain rapport with the individual because many people realize that they are at risk and shape up with this first dialogue. You want to be able to set the tone for continuous improvement and support while setting complete accountability on their shoulders.

A directive tone is carefully controlled and succinct. Be sure that the emphasis is on what you need to see from *them* in order to accept that performance has improved. You must be clear that this must be continuous and positive improvement. Be very careful not to use "weenie words." An example of these words are *sort of, kind of, maybe, try, or* (a really weenie phrase: *"wouldn't it be better or nice if…"*)

Understand that you are doing surgery here. If you work with a sharp scalpel and precise strokes, the patient will heal faster and feel less pain. Inevitably step one fails when managers try to be "too nice." Make your point and then ask for clarification of understanding.

Ask what they heard, how they will accomplish it, what they will do next. Clarify any vague language. If they use words like, *"I'll try to do better."* INVESTIGATE. CLARIFY!

- What *specifically* will you "try?"

- What does "better" mean *specifically?*

They can <u>hide</u> in vague terminology and you'll find yourself going to STEP 2. There are only four reasons you end up in Step 2:

1. You were not direct.

2. You did not clarify gaining understanding and commitment.

3. They don't fit the job.

4. They have already given up or burnt out.

The Process – Step 2

Step two is first documentation. Speak directly to what you believed the agreements to be. Let the employee know that because you are revisiting this with them that you are going to be making detailed notes this time and will be placing your notes in their .

Be crisp when you point to each agreement. Use language like:

"In our last meeting, we came to three agreements. The first one was your commitment to create your reports by

Thursday close of business. Over the last two weeks, I received one on Friday afternoon and the second one on Monday after work hours. This is not acceptable. Do you remember why this was important to me?"

Here you are checking for awareness and whether they even logged the conversation. Sometimes they don't. Realize that if *you* have done *too much talking* in Step One this can be a significant outcome. This is one of the reasons I recommended reviewing "Setting Expectations." They must do the talking to do the integration and processing! So if you are at Step Two ask the questions and then let them draw the distinctions. They must come up with a solution that is acceptable to you and *they must* own it.

Be sure to ask the *specifying questions* so that they are clear and succinct on precise activities that will create the correct results. Check to see if they feel these tasks will provide the best outcome.

The Process – Step 3

If you did not get the results the employee promised in Step 2, you must move to the next step and produce the written performance improvement plan (PIP.) Make sure to connect with Human Resources/Personnel (HR) before proceeding in this step. They may have a pre-approved form that you must use or suggestions to support you in the process. You will also want a representative at the meeting to observe the presentation of the PIP. This is pretty standard and a nice safeguard for you.

I like having an HR representative there to observe and clarify as the PIP is discussed and agreements are reached. As you are talking with HR be sure to understand their rules for timing on the PIP. Some organizations have limits on the amount of time allowed for results. Other organizations leave the timing to the manager. The rule I have used is to shorten the time incrementally depending on the following factors:

- Commitment to the work
- Skill level
- Observed desire to be a part of the team

Some examples of this might be a person with very high technical skill that has been a proven team player but seems to have lost their sense of direction or commitment. If you are pretty sure that they will turn around when they see how serious the situation is then give them more time, up to 60 days.

On the other hand, if you have found that they are really not committed, have an attitude toward the team and not making any attempt to use or improve skills, then give less time. Chances are they have already mentally 'quit' the job and prolonging the decision makes everyone more uncomfortable. Depending on the advice of HR, you may give as little as two weeks.

The reasoning behind the timeframes is to provide ample time for improvement for people you believe can and want to make the shift and to shorten the pain for those that really need to leave. HR will advise you on the wording so that you will have the ability to make a quick decision should the need arise. You will also have language in the PIP that allows for extensions should they make a positive turn around.

If you see improvement during the two week period, meet with the employee (along with HR) and acknowledge the progress. You may allow an extension to the PIP and set new performance objectives to continue the development. Keep the new objectives within the bounds of the original requests and updates with the employee should be made every two weeks until you are confident that the new behavior is set. This might take 6-8 weeks (3-4 meetings.) You will determine the time frame and outcomes.

When writing the PIP there are some standard rules. While HR will have their own form, consider these criteria for effective delivery.

- State the nature of the issues. If there are several issues, look for primary concerns and commonalities. Do not use a 'shotgun' approach to fix everything. Better to address the most important item first and save some of the ancillary ones for continued correction through the Performance Appraisal process.
    - o Example: Punctuality is the common issue and is showing up on status reports, project delivery schedules, etc. Therefore, the identified primary issue is punctuality. Then you list the factual data that supports and points to what you need from the employee. Address each item separately. Again, limit the list but be specific.
- Be factual.

- o Example: Status reports are due each Thursday no later than 3:00 p.m. Status reports for the last 12 weeks have been as much as 4 days overdue and have impacted the department project plans, delaying critical test schedules and product marketing plans.
- State the expectations for improvement. Be clear and concise. Be very specific as to time, quality and quantity.
  - o Example: Immediate improvement is required. Status reports must be delivered to the supervisor no later than 3:00 p.m. All specifics must be recorded as to project delays, successes and performance criteria for testing purposes.
- State the time factor for this performance plan.
  - o Example: This performance improvement plan is in effect immediately. Results are to be monitored for a period of two months. All items detailed above will be examined by your supervisor for quality, timeliness and completeness. Any items not meeting required standards will lead to further disciplinary actions, up to and including termination of employment. At the end of the probationary period this performance plan will be filed for the annual performance evaluation. If the criteria identified in this PIP has been met through the remainder of the year; this document will be removed from the file. (NOTE: Any and all of this language and process should be reviewed by HR or your legal counsel for nuances of your state employment laws.)

- o It is also wise to state that performance of these items is to be continuous. It must be sustained throughout the term of employment.
- Any follow up should also be stated. How often will you review and monitor their performance? What will this look like?
- Signature blocks should be provided for you as supervisor administering the PIP, a witness (usually HR) and for acknowledgement by the employee. There should also be a place for the date since this is a time sensitive document.

The Process – Step 4

The last phase is termination of employment. When you have issued the PIP, monitored performance and found that they are still not actively meeting the criteria, proceed to HR with the request for termination. No discussion is required with the employee at this point until HR is ready to proceed. If you are in a small company with no full-time HR and no legal staff, be sure to check any employment contract that was signed when the employee was hired. Usually the employment contracts are very simple and termination with cause is already stated in the PIP.

Prepare ahead of time to have someone witness the termination (you may be the witness if HR is going to deliver the news.) Prepare to have someone pack the personal belongings of the employee (you, another manager or security may do this or someone from HR.) The packing should be done while the termination meeting is happening. Be sure to be discreet about this and allow maximum respect for the individual's belongings.

Termination is best done early in the day so that you do not prolong your anxiety. Keep the message concise. I frequently use phrasing like:

"John, you and I have had several discussions to date regarding the necessity for your performance improvement. During the last 2 weeks you have been expected to turn in the status reports and project updates on time. This has not happened. You may word this in several ways, "it has become necessary to make a decision. That decision is to terminate your employment." or "based on your decision to not meet the requirements", or "based on your failure to meet the requirements", I'm terminating your employment." It's tough but there are no 'weenie-words' and it acknowledges that the total fault is theirs. You don't want to leave any room for the employee to leave saying "Boy, look what those guys at my last job did to me." Termination usually results in some 'after-the-fact' communication with an official governmental agency (unemployment, workforce commission, etc.) to establish the facts of the termination. You want to be very clear here.

Making this short and direct is less painful for you and the employee. HR should have all necessary forms and recommendations ready to discuss with the employee. If there is room for further conversation I always spend some time letting the employee know that I see them as a good person with skills that may be better suited to another job. If I felt like they were trying but ill suited to the job then I would tell them that I would be a referral for *other* types of work. I have to feel that they really have the desire and work ethic to make this offer so I always did it carefully. However, the emphasis is always on the fact that they did not fit *this* job. This leaves them with a measure of self-respect and helps them focus on what they *can and like to do.*

What to do if they get emotional.

It is important to understand that there is plenty of opportunity for emotion in this process. First let's look at the emotion you may have in the process and how to handle it most effectively.

The first piece is to realize that this is tough for most people. You may have feelings about their lack of compliance or about putting someone out of a job. Realize that these are just emotions; reactions to a situation. These feelings are generated by our very active imaginations and supported by our past experiences. And as human beings we should have some emotion at this point. Managers cannot become calloused; even in situations like these.

When working with clients on issues such as this, I use many ways to help them look at what these feelings are and how to support them. When I say "just" emotions, I do not mean to minimize their impact. I do mean that we have "choice" in how we handle them. It never feels like it while we are in the grip of these emotions. When I teach classes on emotional intelligence the objective is to help people understand how to identify the emotion and then deal with their responses in a more resourceful way, Understanding where emotions come from within us and how to support and use them in a beneficial way is important. When you have your own self-awareness about emotions and how they make you react, you will be better able to help the employee work through theirs.

The first stage is to realize what emotions you are experiencing. One way to do this is to use the model for exploring emotions .

Exploring Emotions: (Complete these statements.)
1. *When I think about…*
2. *I feel…*
3. *I then think…*
4. *That makes me want to…*

As you answer these you will find definition about the issue and the emotion you hold about it. Consider this next question carefully.
5. *What am I attached to?*

This is an incredibly powerful question. My clients frequently tell me "nothing" as their first answer. That is seldom the case. In as little as 1% of the cases the answer is nothing. In 99% of the time, we want something to occur or show up in a certain way. The reason we are upset is because it is not happening the <u>way</u> we wanted and <u>now we are attached to a limited outcome.</u>

Now look at the next question thoughtfully.
6. *What would happen if I allowed a different outcome? OR What would happen if it didn't matter what showed up?*

If you allow yourself to lease these ideas for a while, you will find that you have many more options and are relaxing about the outcome.

Now answer from this place of resourcefulness:
   7. *I have made the right decision for myself and (the employee.) Now how do I help them leave with honor?*

Throughout these questions you have been supporting yourself and not suppressing your emotions. This is important. In business we are asked to put our feelings on the shelf: to keep a stiff upper lip, to be strong and not show our emotions.

The interesting part of that is how *unhealthy* it is. Your adrenal glands start working overtime, blood pumping furiously and heart rate increasing…and there's no outlet. We put a stopper on it. Where is all of that going to go? What happens when you shake up a bottle of carbonated liquid? Look at all that energy. Now put a cork in it! Over time the liquid will lose its fizz and so will you or in extreme cases, the bottle may explode.

Learn to work with emotions. Realize this is a natural body response. They are not good or bad. You don't have to get shaken up at every turn. You can learn to work with them in effective and, frankly, very powerful ways, becoming more and more resourceful over time. (For more information, you can contact Strategic Transformations at info@strategictransformations.net for our EQ^2 program or for our Coaching Emotional Intelligence program.)

When working with the employee and you see them getting emotional, acknowledge that you realize this is very hard on them. Tell them that you had hoped for a better outcome as well. Let them know that HR will let them know any and all support that is available to them (which may include unemployment insurance, medical insurance through COBRA (or some company funding,) and in some cases severance pay.) Let HR give them the details.

If they are becoming angry, *pace and lead* them. You do this by slowing your voice pattern, speaking softer (more quietly) and breathing deeply. I have even held up my hands in the sports signal for Time Out and said, "Let's take a breath here." "Just take a moment and breathe, we are here to support you through this."

Some employees may cry. Have tissues handy and give them a few moments to become calm. Being gentle and supportive is important and again acknowledges that you are aware of how difficult this must be. Tell them to take their time and even offer them a few minutes by stepping out to get them a drink of water. Compassion is the key in this situation. Be aware that men can cry as well as women. The pressures of business and family can overcome anyone.

Allow them whatever measure of control you can give them at this point. Ask what they might need to support them. Ask if they have any questions. Ask them if they would like private time with HR to answer their questions. All of this helps them feel empowered to take back their life. The more direct and compassionate you are at this point the easier it will be for them.

Their emotions will come from several directions (sometimes all at once.)

1. They may worry about what others will think. *Reassure them that this is a private matter and will not be discussed with anyone.*
2. They may wonder about their personal effects. *Reassure them that they have been packed up discreetly and will be brought to them.*
3. They may have a lot of questions about how this will affect their career, job hunt, etc. *If you feel that you could honestly be a reference for them for something other than the work they have done for you (a different career) and HR is okay with it, then offer this. HR may choose to field this question so let them take the lead.*
4. They may worry about what to tell their spouse. *HR may allow them to call into the Employee Assistance Program if that is available in your company. This will allow them to talk with a counselor and address their concerns effectively.*

The critical part of this is to understand that emotions are not good or bad. It is our decisions about them or our lack of support for them that make them difficult. Allow space to express them. Allow time to work through them. See each other as valuable human beings going through a difficult time. Even the best of us have been fired or laid off. We have survived, grown and been even more successful because of the incident *if* we have used it as a learning experience.

Closing

After you have finished delivering the news, have a signal with HR to let you know when it is best to leave. Express to the employee that you wish them the best and that HR will answer any remaining questions or concerns. Let them know that you will be sure that their possessions are delivered to the room discreetly in a few minutes. Then leave quietly and allow HR to proceed with the final issues such as collecting badges, passwords, etc.

In Conclusion

With luck you will not have to terminate many people in your career but the higher you go and the longer your career, the more you will face the PIP process. Learning to communicate clearly, effectively and frequently with employees will help you visit the PIP less often. Understand that almost everyone at some point in their professional life ends up in a job that does not fit their skills, interests or values. When this happens the sooner we realize it and are supported in finding something that does suit, the easier it is for everyone.

Remember the analogy of the doctor. Being direct, honest, and clear is like a masterful surgeon. It is less painful for the employee and for you if you use a quick, masterful stroke to make the cut.

Integration Scenario:

Note: In this scenario, it is not to be assumed that these are the only conversations taking place between the manager and employee. These are the targeted conversations around the specific issue.

Day One:

Catherine was concerned. Tom had been a great employee for over three years. He had steadily been promoted and was now working as a project lead for the testing and integration group. As a lead he was required to create reports on testing results and projections and status reports that fed back into the project plan.

Catherine had been hearing from the project manager that testing results had not been formally reported for two weeks and Tom had to be prompted consistently just to get the verbal reports. He also had missed turning in the last status report and was 4 days late on the previous one. While he had never gotten any of these in on time since he took the position, it was now at a critical point. The project manager was very upset and wanted Catherine to do something now. Some of the modular tests were holding up results for integration testing.

Catherine had talked with Tom last week when she called him in for the status report update. Tom had seemed illusive about the reasons for his' delay and never answered the real issue of when he would turn it in. Because Catherine had always seen Tom as a good employee and had supported making him a project lead, she hoped this conversation would fix the problem. Now the PM was in her office with another problem with Tom's delivery status. Catherine knew she had to set the expectations.

Catherine called Tom to come to her office.

Tom enters with a frown, "I know this is about those reports and I'd get them done if everyone would just leave me alone."

This was unlike the old Tom and Catherine was surprised by this outburst. "Tom, it is about the lateness of the reports but I'm sensing that this is a big problem for you and it is important to get to the heart of this. What's keeping you from a timely response?"

"Look, I'm doing the best I can. It's not easy to crunch the data and fill in all the reports. This isn't fun and I'm doing it as fast as I can." Tom said with a raised voice.

"I can hear that this is not fun for you. You are very upset right now and I'm trying to hear what the issues are. Can you be more specific about the process and what's holding you up?" Catherine noticed that she was feeling tight and took a deep breath, determined not to get sucked into his tension.

"Look, I have to get the test results from all three shifts and then put them in the spreadsheet. Then I have to read through the charts and make a decision on how much longer it will take or what's not functioning up to criteria. Then I've got to get that to Rick. He always seems to want more data. Then I'm supposed to write that stupid status report and make up stuff to tell management. It's never ending." Tom said tightly.

"Tom, this isn't like you. What's really going on here? You have always pulled data on our projects. You used to volunteer to do the spreadsheet and analysis work. Am I right?" Catherine asked.

Tom sat silently for a minute. "Yeah, I used to do it and it was fun."

"What's different now?" Catherine asked.

"I don't know it's just different and I hate it." Tom replied.

"Tom, do you dislike being a project lead?" Catherine asked.

"No, I like being a lead. It's important for my career. I just don't like the deadlines," he replied.

"Tom, we've always worked under deadlines. You've always been the best at pushing the tests through and getting everything done on time and frequently before time. What's changed? What specifically about doing this as a project lead is setting you off?" she pushed gently.

"I don't know. I just feel pressured from all angles. I don't feel comfortable writing down my decisions. I'm not sure I'm right or what impact it will have on the project," he answered.

"So what you are most concerned about is the decision process and the impact to others?" she queried.

"Yeah, I guess that's it," he said without commitment.

"Tom, have you talked with Rick about this? Has he explained what he does with the data and decisions?" she asked,

"No, he's usually just hassling me to get the reports done," he replied.

"Would it help if I facilitated a conversation with the two of you?" she asked.

"No, I'll do it," he replied. But Catherine noted that he did not have much conviction.

"Tom, I'm concerned. What's important to me is that the reports get in on time with your best thoughts and recommendations. When the reports are late it holds up other decisions down the line. You are going to make some bad calls. Everyone does. If you are concerned with your decision, sit down with Rick and tell him where your decision is stretched. The timeliness of these reports is a job requirement for the project lead position. Now what I want you to tell me is what's important to you?" she said.

"I want to do a good job. I want to make sure that no one can point a finger at me and say that I screwed up the project." Tom said.

"Tom, no one person can make that big a difference if we are working together as a team. You are having a larger negative impact by not doing the reports on time. I have two possible suggestions that I want you to consider: One, I want you to pull the data, put it in the spreadsheet, print out the charts and sit down with Rick and discuss with him how you would make your decisions. Let him coach you on what he sees as critical and for areas of agreement. Then ask all the questions you can think of to understand what he needs. You can then create the report and once again review it with Rick. When both of you are satisfied then move on to the status report. You know it's just a summary of the larger report and I use it for the staff briefing and for the financial planning.

The second suggestion is only to be used if you still hate the job. I want you to consider what else you rather do. You are a valuable part of the team and I don't want you driving yourself nuts over something you don't like. Do these two ideas make sense to you?" She counseled.

"Yeah, they make sense and I'll talk with Rick. Thanks for caring." Tom said.

"I'll look forward to your report on Friday. What time can I expect it?" She asked.

"I know," he said with a grin, "3;00 p.m., right?"

Catherine smiled, "3:00 p.m. it is then."

Catherine later checked with Rick and heard that Tom had come to him for a very good conversation. Catherine was glad that was behind her.

Two weeks later:

Two weeks later, the problem was the same if not worse! Catherine called Tom in to her office.

Tom walked in with a chip on his shoulder and slumped in the chair next to her.

"Tom, what's up? Rick was in here and said that you had been really angry with him about the report. He said you were three days late and had really let him have it when he asked about the report." Catherine asked.

"I've had it up to here with Mr. Goody-goody." Tom groused.
"What do you mean?" she asked.

"He's just Mr. Perfect, that's all. He's always on time. Always knows everything. I'm sick of working with him." Tom said angrily.

"What specifically has Rick done to make you so angry?" she asked.

"He wants everything down to the minute. He wants all the data analysis done and on his desk at 10:00 a.m. every Tuesday, no questions asked." Tom growled.

"Tom, that's always been the deadline for Rick's report. Do you know why he needs it by 10:00?" she asked.

"Yeah, he says he has to pull it all together for a 1:00 meeting on Tuesday afternoon." He replied.

"That doesn't give him much time to pull your report and six others together, does it?" she asked.

"It's plenty of time. He can always work on the others reports. If I bring it in by noon, he slide my stuff in easily." He frowned.

"Tom, first, I don't think you are being fair to Rick. He needs time to analyze the affects of each of your reports and put a recommendation and timeline together for the project meeting. He also has the right to have lunch, doesn't he?" she queried.

"Yeah, I guess." He said.

"Second, the other leads turn in their reports at 9:00 a.m. For some reason Rick seems to be cutting you some slack. Why is that?" she asked.

Tom looked surprised. "I didn't know that."

"It's true. I'm surprised by the leniency of that deadline also. In my book that's very nice of Rick. That means he is working on the others' reports while you take extra time to do your report.

"Did you have your meeting with Rick as I suggested last time we met?" she asked.

"Yeah, it helped. It made it easier to do the report." Tom said, still thinking about the timeline surprise.

"Then what's going on? What specifically is delaying your report?" Catherine asked.

"I just don't seem to get around to it until the last minute." He said.

"Tom, do you have this on your calendar as a required activity?" she questioned.

"Yeah," he said.

"Do your people get you their data on time?" Catherine asked.

"Yeah, they are a good team." He said.

"Then what's the problem?" She asked.

"I don't know I guess I just don't like doing it." He said.

"Tom, that's not good enough. Last time we discussed that this was a condition of the job. It is a requirement. The timeliness of this report and the status report is critical to the business and is the sole responsibility of the project lead. It comes down to do you want to do the lead role or do you want to do something else in the department?" she laid it out clearly.

"I want the job. I just don't like doing the report." Tom said.

"There are parts of every job that we don't like but that must be done. It comes with the job. This report comes with the lead position. Out of all you do, this is job number one. The status report is job number two. It is your responsibility and if it is not what you want to do then we'll move you elsewhere. Is there anything preventing you from doing this job?" She asked firmly.

"No, I can do it." He said.

"Do you need training on the tools?"

"No," he replied.

"Do you need further coaching on the decision process?" she asked.

"No, I got that from Rick." He said.

"Is there anything else that could prevent you from doing the reports in a timely fashion?" she asked.

"No, I'll do it." He said, but she noted there was not much enthusiasm.

"Tom, you have always been a top performer and for what ever reason, you are choosing not to do this part of the job with your usual top quality. I want you to know that I'm going to document our conversation. I know that you can do this and do it well. If you choose, for any reason, to not do it on time and with the quality I expect, then our next discussion will be more serious. Am I making myself clear?" she clarified.

"Yeah, I understand. I'll do it." Tom answered.

"Tom, are you sure you want this lead position? I don't sense much energy around doing this work." Catherine asked.

"No, I want the job. I'll do it. I don't want to go any place else in the company. I want to work here and do this job." Tom said firmly.

"Are you sure?" she asked.

"Yes, I'm sure." He replied.

"Then I'd like you to tell me what you are going to do differently in your process that will make certain that the reports are done on time and well." Catherine asked for clarification and confirmation that he had thought this through completely.

Tom sat quietly for quite a while. Catherine waited patiently.

"Well, I'll make a note in my to-do list that will give me a reminder to pull the data on Monday afternoon. Then I'll start work on it that day, inputting data and then Tuesday morning I'll put the data together." He said.

"Will that give you enough time to get it in on time?" Catherine asked.

"Yeah, I've been waiting until Tuesday morning but Monday will give me more time." Tom said.

"Then I have your commitment to getting the reports in on time by pulling data on Monday and then finishing the report on Tuesday. You will have the reports in to Rick at what time?" she asked.

"I'll get them in by 10:00." He said.

"Do you understand the consequences of not getting the reports done on time?" she asked.

"Yeah, Rick can't get his evaluation and report done by his 1:00 meeting." He replied.

"That's part of it. What's my next action if these actions don't meet expectations?" she asked.

Tom thought for a minute and then blushed crimson, "You'll have to write me up."

"That's right, Tom. I'll have to do the part of MY job that I don't like. For the good of the organization, I have to do these things. Do you understand what you will put us both through if you fail to get these reports in on time?" she asked without a smile.

Tom gave a small sideways grin and said, "Yeah, it's the axe for me."

"Tom, I don't want to wield and axe with you. I want to see the type of great performance I have come to expect from you. If there is anything else preventing you from doing your job, I want to know. I want to help you be successful. All you have told me so far is that you just don't like doing the reports. You have committed to setting up a reminder system for the project testing analysis. I'd also like for you to commit to a similar system on the status report each Friday." She persisted.

"Yeah, that's the easy one." Tom said.

"I appreciate that you may feel it is easier. That's good. However, it is also late consistently. It is also important to the job as defined. Are we in agreement and full understanding?" she asked.

"Yes, I'll set up the reminders today." He said.

Catherine reminded him that she was going to make notes in his file on this discussion and would expect an immediate improvement. They shook hands and Catherine silently prayed that the improvement would come.

Two weeks later:
Catherine called Tom and asked him to join her in the conference room. Tom said into the phone, "Is this the axe?"

Catherine said, "It's the first step, Tom." She put the phone down with a deep sigh. She looked across the table at the HR manager, Sue and said, "I hate this part of my job."

Sue nodded, "I know. But from what you've told me, you've given him lots of encouragement and counseling. More than I think is necessary sometimes. You even e-mailed him to check on his progress last week and got assurance that it was being done only to find him not delivering. This is his choice at this point."

Tom came through the door and was surprised to see Sue sitting across the round table with Catherine. A low whistle under his breath and a quiet, "You guys are really serious this time, aren't you?"

Catherine looked at him seriously and said, "Tom, I've been serious every time we've talked abut this. I thought you knew that."

"Yeah, well…yeah, I did. I just hoped it wouldn't come to this. Am I being fired?" Tom asked.

"No and I hope it won't come to that. However, I am putting you on formal written notice. I've asked Sue to come and be a witness to our conversation. I have also asked her to stay after our conversation in case there is something you have not felt comfortable telling me. This is very serious, Tom, and I don't want there to be any reason missed for your not performing to the requirements of the job. Understood?" Catherine asked.

"This is sounding worse and worse." Tom said.
"Tom, I believe you CAN meet these expectations. I hope this is the last counseling conversation we need. It is critical that you understand that the timeliness and quality of the reports expected from a Project Lead are the number one priority for this job. We have had this dialogue before, right?" she asked for agreement.

Tom said, "Yeah, several times."

"Then here is what this performance document calls for…" Catherine goes through the complete document, pausing to check for understanding and agreement at each critical point. She reviews with Tom the action plan that he had suggested last time and what needed to be done to make the reports' deadlines.

Tom, once again, assured her that he could do the job and made some adjustments to the action plan. Catherine then reaffirmed that the next action could be termination. There were no second chances from this point on.

She signed both copies and asked for Tom's signature to signify that he had been fully informed of the plan. After signing, Catherine asked Sue to witness the document. Catherine then handed one copy to Tom and told him that he was free to stay and talk with Sue. He declined and said he had work to do.

Catherine encouraged him as he left, "Tom, I know you can do this. You've done great in the past, do it now."

"Yeah, I better." He said and shut the door quietly.

Catherine made a copy of the document for her files and gave Sue the originals. She sighed as she had earlier and told Sue she really hoped he would pull out of this. "He was a good performer and could be again," she said as she handed Sue the document.

Sue patted her shoulder and said, "It's his choice and always has been. If he wants to do it he will. You've offered to move him and he declined. It's up to him now. You've done the best you can do for him."

The first week Tom was right on time with everything. The second week he was an hour late with the Tuesday reports and did not send in his status until after lunch on Friday. The third week, Catherine called Sue and planned the termination process. He'd miss the Tuesday deadline completely and turned in the report AFTER Rick's 1:00 meeting with no explanations or support for Rick.

Thursday morning as Tom came into work, Catherine met him at the elevator.

"Tom, please come with me." Catherine asked her heart racing but her face calm.

287

"This is it, isn't it?" Tom asked quietly.

"Yes, Sue is waiting for us in the conference room." She said.

"Should I go clear out my desk?" Tom asked.

Catherine gave a quiet, sad smile and said, "We've already done that for you before anyone else arrived this morning. We wanted to make this as easy as possible for you." With that they entered the conference room.

The discussion was short. Tom knew the reason and said that maybe this was the right thing. He was really tired of the job and maybe he'd find something else that would be more interesting for him. He thanked Catherine for the chance and for her counseling. Sue took over to fill out the final paperwork and to collect badges, passwords, etc.

Catherine left the room feeling like she'd failed but then she realized, "Tom really didn't want the job and wasn't willing to let me move him. This was his choice. For whatever reason, he was ready to leave. I did the right thing for the department and that's my job. I don't like doing it," and then thinking of what Tom had said about doing the reports, "but it is my job. At least I gave him several chances and he made the choice. I'll miss him but it's the right thing to do. I'd have hurt many more people and the project if I'd ignored the problem." With a big sigh, Catherine went back to her office and called Rick to make arrangements for next week's reports and planning.

Lessons Learned:

1. What were the three most important steps in your estimation to the performance process?

2. What was important about the dialogue between Catherine and Tom?

3. What might you have done more of, better or differently?

4. What results would you expect from your changes?

5. What stops most managers from taking these performance steps?

6. What would help you take the necessary steps in a timely fashion?

7. What are the critical steps required by your company?

8. What did learn that surprised you?

9. What parts of this lesson will help you most in the future?

10. On a scale of one to ten (with 10 being best,) how direct are you in a performance conversation?

11. What were the soft words (like sort of, maybe)?

12. How many of them do you hear yourself saying in a normal conversation?

13. How often do you use them in a performance conversation?

14. What else can you use from this lesson in other management or planning discussions?

Chapter 14
Managing Group Dynamics

Establishing guidelines for improving relationships within your organization can create a better working environment and set inherent ground rules for use when times become difficult. Several issues are usually in play when morale begins to deteriorate or dysfunctional behavior becomes evident.

The intention of improving the whole so that each individual can be more productive and eventually happier in the work place is paramount to the success of this venture.

Management must hold a clear intention and remind themselves frequently that this is ultimately the way to make their job easier and have a happy, successful organization. It is always a plus in business when the management team is adept at providing support. When leaders are confident as challenges erupt and opinions become more strident the team actually relaxes knowing that there is someone at the helm who can guide them through the storm.

If this has not been a strength within the organization, you will be overcoming distrust and a lack of respect. An important thing to remember is that this did not happen overnight and will not cure itself immediately.

Rule to Remember:

Persistence, patience and understanding will be your cornerstones as you begin to rebuild and enhance the performance of your team.

The Basics

Initial communication is a key part of the process. Meeting individually with staff is a critical piece of the strategy. Staffing issues usually arise because there is no process for venting or feedback through the organization. You will frequently hear staff refer to lack of management response or interest. This does not mean that the leadership is not hearing employee issues, only that the feedback loop is broken or "I am not getting quality time."

Learning to have effective one-on-one conversations and bringing a clear communication to the employee will make a big difference in the way they work with others as well as you, their manager. Preparing for one-on-one meetings, having a plan for follow-up and setting future guidelines for behavior, feedback and expectations is essential to your success.

The Intention

If there is stress in the organization then talking with your people will uncover much of the problem. Your intention is to hear them; not judge them. Tell yourself throughout the process, "This is not about me. This is for the good of the organization." The more open you stay to the issues, without becoming embroiled in them or seeing them as a threat to your management style or process, the faster you will resolve the issues. Every time your people offer information, it is a rare opportunity for you *and your employee* to create new solutions. Hold this intention and you will be far ahead of any other manager in your organization.

Session Structure and Process

Various processes drive the exact structure used, however many sessions follow a basic formula that can be customized based on the employee and the issues to be discussed.

Pre-session Planning

- Let the employees know ahead of time (in a staff meeting) that you plan one-on-one meetings with each of them. Set the stage for improvement of relationships and teaming. Set times for each employee and stress that these meetings are important and that you are looking forward to their input.
- If this is a unique experience in your office (not done before or not done in a very long time,) let the

employees know that you have been reviewing your management style and the organization and you know that things need to shift to get better. Transitions and process changes are always a good lead in but do not have to be in place for this to be effective.

- Imagine several scenarios for how the conversations might play out, and how you might respond. Evaluating these scenarios with your management team and your coach/consultant is an effective way to prepare ahead.
- Make a "talking points" memo to refer to specific issues that need to be addressed so that you are not lost in the conversation.
- Consider effective questions to be asked that will support your conversation and awaken the employee to more awareness of the business and his/her contribution.
- Send a meeting notice with opening questions and your initial thoughts to help the employee prepare and be in the right mindset for the dialogue. (See Session Opening for suggestions.)

Session Opening

The first step is for you to answer these questions prior to the meeting. You will then have a solid context for the meeting and will appear congruent.

- What is the importance of this meeting? What's important to you?
- What are you trying to accomplish (improving morale, better understanding of staff and their issues, better teamwork, etc.?)
- What atmosphere do you wish to create in the

> meeting (building or improving relationship, get to know staff, set ideas for new management style, etc.?)
> - What are the key topics to be addressed?
>   - What are the business dependencies (big picture?) What would you like for your staff to understand about the business that they might not realize now?

Letting the employee know what to expect helps set the stage for a successful discussion by ensuring that everyone has the same basic understanding of the purpose and agenda.

Choose a conference room or if you must have it in your office, be sure to sit with the employee, not behind a desk or table. Create an atmosphere that is open and relaxing and as neutral as possible. This will psychologically create more opportunity for dialogue.

Explain the process of working together

As the employee joins you for the meeting, thank them for their time. Let them know that you are looking forward to gaining and sharing new insights with them. Tell them you have created some notes for you to keep a focused conversation and you will be referring to them to stay on track. However, you also want to assure them that you are open to whatever they would like to talk about because this is their meeting too.

Understanding the types and profiles of the employee is always a nice to know and can be covered quickly with your coach/consultant or refer back to the lesson Building High Performance Teams for personality styles. This will help you in understanding the needs of the employee in their conversational style.

Detail oriented people will have more questions and concerns about the reason for the meeting or will want to delve into the "why's" behind your questions. They will also give you more detail in their answers to your questions *or they may be very inhibited in responding* if they are not sure what the purpose is behind your questions.

Your very social people or the drivers in your organization will run with whatever question you ask with little or no detail. You may need to ask more specific questions to get the information you need to evaluate issues in the group or process. Knowing your staff and their styles will help you be more effective in communicating with them.

Rules and Tools: Consider Options

Request that the employee consider new alternatives to critical behaviors. Encourage the employee to share new ideas, suggestions and anecdotes to help stimulate thinking about new ways to address the issues.

Focus the discussion

Narrow the focus of the conversation to a topic that can realistically be covered in the time available.

For one-on-one's to be effective a limited scope is important. This is a temperature check that is needed at least once a quarter to determine how successful staff are feeling in their jobs; to determine whether there are any issues that are not being addressed among staff; and whether there is need for process change or group intervention is required. Create your talking points or list of questions to focus on these topics or specific issues you are seeing in the group. It is also a terrific time to build their critical thinking skills about how the business runs and what the goals of the organization need to be to reach success.

For a first time one-on-one, consider questions like this:
1. *How do you feel about our organization?*
2. *What does this group do that makes it successful?*
3. *What is your understanding of the goals of our organization?*
4. *What would you change if you could?*
5. *What issues would you like for me to be aware of?*
6. *What stops you from being as successful as you'd like to be?*

Each of these questions allows an open-ended conversation and will encourage the employee to give you real insight into how they feel about working with the group or with the process of the organization. You do not have to ask all of them. Choose two or three for the first session or make up your own. Be sure they are *effective questions* so that you create a strong, positive dialogue with your employee. The first objective in these one-on-one meetings is to create a better relationship and understanding of how your organization is working as a whole. Remember you are doing a temperature check and will build a plan from the overall dialogue with your staff.

NOTE: It is best to use the same questions for each employee so that you have a benchmark for the whole organization. If you wander through the one-on-one meetings with a variety of questions, you will not have a good understanding of the present state of affairs. You will also not be able to get a clear indication of what specifically needs to be addressed.

If you have done one-on-one meetings in the past or for the follow-on conversations, you can still use the previous questions or you can begin to drive to a new level with staff to build their *critical thinking skills*. Consider these example questions:

1. *What would make this organization more successful?*
2. *If you were president (Executive Director, CEO) of this business (or organization) what would you see as success? What would be most important for you to see as a quarterly/annual objective for this group?*
3. *How could we reach that success?*
4. *What would you suggest to improve our current processes?*
5. *If you were a customer of our organization, what do you think we do well? What makes that important to you? What would you want to see more of, better or different? What else?*

As you can see these questions put the <u>responsibility on them</u> to determine how the business is or should be run. We are building ***critical thinking*** skills into the employee so that later they can draw their own lines on the map and be in sync with the organizational goals.

If they are not able to make the connection then ***directive*** conversation can be used. But understand that *"telling"* has little or no impact on people. The true changes come from their decisions about their behaviors. The more you create a *learning process* for them the faster they will change their behavior. When they suggest new ways of working with others or the current process, ask for benefits, outcomes and what else? Go deeper to increase learning for both of you.

What to do if they get emotional?

If the employee comes in with a chip on their shoulder, acting fearful or very stressed, be sure to set them at ease. This is new or different for both of you and the meeting is important to help change the current working environment. You are looking for their input.

If they continue to be emotional the **most important thing** for you is to remain calm. Remember, the emotion is *not about you* (even if they are challenging or angry at you.) The emotion is their *perception. It always comes from some fear or insecurity.* When you go back to your *intention* you will see that you are not out to attack them (no matter what they think,) and they are only hurting themselves. Ask yourself: If this were me, what would I want to have happen right now or be said right now? The important part is to keep your intention clear and realize emotion usually comes from fear!

Rules and tools: Closing

Consider how the employee can synthesize the
information session.

Bring closure to the session by:
- **asking for feedback,**
- **drawing conclusions,**
- **identifying next steps,**
- **Or simply sharing information about the experience of the session.**

Always close the session by *thanking them* for being so open to exploring more effective ways to work with their team and you. Tell them you plan to support them by noticing every instance where you see them bringing these new behaviors into the workplace. This will let them know you:
- **Support them and want them to be more successful.**
- **Will be observing behaviors.**
- **Have expectations for their improvement.**

In Conclusion

Notice: your primary function was to develop the key *talking points* and then ask *effective questions* to draw out the employee and their opinions and suggestions. It was your intention to learn more about the organization, its successes and challenges. When you do regularly scheduled one-on-one meetings, you not only know your organization well but you have a baseline for the health of the organization. Checking the temperature and making necessary adjustments as you go through the year.

The next step is to create a feedback session to support your awareness from the meetings.

- Make notes on what you learned from this and share with your management team
- Create effective next steps (an action plan for improvements.)
- When will you bring the group together as a whole?
- In what context will you create the gathering?
- What feedback is relevant?
- What objectives will let the team know that you heard them and are willing to honor their suggestions and support their challenges?
- What guidelines do you now feel are essential to improving the team and their collaboration and support?
- AND BREATHE a sigh of relief (for a job well-done!)

Integration Scenario:

Donna is a second line manager for a large group and she is meeting with John and Jessica who report to her as first line managers. Donna, John and Jessica are all in agreement that morale is low due to a recent transition. They have determined to use the strategies of one-on-ones to meet with their groups. Donna would like a detailed game plan to be sure that all possible scenarios are supported in the organization. Their plan looks like this:

1. Donna will come to both John's and Jessica's staff meetings. She will offer words of encouragement that the transition was tough but that she knows these teams have tremendous talent and flexibility. She will set the tone to be supportive and empathetic to the stress of change but set expectations that each team has the capability to develop strong processes for the new world.

2. John and Jessica, respectively, will spend a few moments asking the team for comments on what went well in the transition. Then they will ask what the team would like to see done more of, better or different in the future so that they will feel better supported.

3. John and Jessica will then set the stage for the one-on-one meetings to have a more individual conversation with team members. They will also establish a time for each individual team to get back together for a feedback session.

4. John has determined that there are two people on his team who are not happy with the transition and are even creating negativity in the group. He's not looking forward to the conversations but knows that not speaking to these team members will create even more unrest. His plan for the discussions is as follows:

a. See where their strengths are. Look at the things that they do well and how each supports the team. Have this list in front of him so that he can refer to it from time to time.

b. Establish what's important to John and the team. Pick one or two things that are critical success factors and be prepared to articulate why they are important.

c. Establish how they are not currently meeting this objective. Be clear, concise and keep it factual. This is not about John or John's feelings. This is about delivery. The more factual John is in representing what he sees as important to the team, the less likely employees will become defensive.

d. Check in on what's important to them. Give them an opportunity to express what they need.

e. Keep them focused on delivery not feelings or excuses. What can they do to meet these objectives?

f. Do they see anything that might stop them from doing what they say they will do?

g. What could they do even more of, better or different?

h. What check points or feedback loops would help them stay on track?

i. Let them know they are supported in being successful.

j. Congratulate them on being so positive in the discussion and thank them for supporting John and the team.

k. Preparation for emotional response:

    i. Allow their emotions but don't get involved. "This is not about me."

    ii. Assume they have talents and abilities; let's use those strengths to get back on track.

    iii. Be quiet if it gets heated. Allow them to vent and wait for them to calm down.

    iv. Reiterate that this is for the good of the organization and it is imperative that we all work together.

    v. Allow them to gain control of their emotions and then ask to continue.

    vi. Have tissues available.

    vii. Make notes to capture what they will need or do differently and how they will provide feedback.

l. Take notes immediately following each meeting to capture ways to improve the organization and to provide feedback to larger group.

m. Make notes on follow-up for individual commitments.

n. Set plan for group meeting.

5. After all individual meetings are held Donna, John and Jessica meet to share insights and plan for delivering feedback to larger groups. Topics:

    a. Where did they find they have agreement?

    b. What are they doing well?

    c. What could they do even better?

    d. What would create even more momentum with staff?

    e. Create a way to celebrate what they used to do and kick-start a new way of working together.

    f. Send out meeting notice for follow up with groups.

Notice:

- The overall planning to insure success.

- The follow-up and feedback.

- That John had plans for both good and potentially heated meetings with staff.

Being prepared creates more confidence and will allow you to be flexible as the need arises. Playing the scenario in your head and planning your contingencies ahead of time will solve 90% of your problems before they ever occur.

Terah Stearns

Lessons Learned:

1. What 3 things did you like most in the planning process? How will it help you overcome issues?

2. What staff issues do you wish to address first?

3. What is your focus?

4. What would success look like after the sessions? What are you trying to accomplish?

5. What questions did you find in the lesson that would be most helpful to you with your staff?

6. How might you change them to elicit even better response or create more clarity for your staff or your situation?

7. Consider your present staff: Which ones might be more antagonistic in the session?

8. What do you want them to understand is most important to you (or your organization?) How will you state this in a powerful, positive way?

9. What is the "big picture" that you want your staff to realize? What 3 things could you say or do that would help them see their role more clearly in the success of this big picture?

10. What is your follow-up plan for the team?

Terah Stearns

Conclusion

You may have read through the book quickly; picking a stray thought or two about the processes described. Some of you may have taken each chapter to heart and tried the ideas in the context of your business. No matter what your method of studying this book, I know that it will have spoken to you at a deeper level. That has been my intention in writing this book.

As a coach, trainer, speaker and consultant, I have had the great challenge and amazing opportunity to work with many companies. Each has had its compelling and unique stories and each has provided a basis for a chapter or two in this book. The stories you have read in the integration scenarios are a synthesis of many years of experience and I hope you now realize that no matter what business you are in, your *people* are the power and potential within your business.

When your employees buy in, they will help you drive any outcome to a successful conclusion. Feel free to contact me if you would like more information or support in the processes described. There is nothing like a supportive and

310

a committed partner in your success. I truly believe that *together, we succeed.* I have a passion for business, people, success and abundance. I believe that we all deserve the best and that we can do anything when we band together in common goals.

You know the power of negativity. Now you can *imagine the power* of unleashing positive potential in your organization and through the exercises in this book, *you can do it!*

I look forward to hearing your success stories and invite you to contact me at terah@strategictransformations.net. Check out our website at www.strategictransformations.net for more products and information or to sign up for our tips and techniques bulletins.

Together, we succeed.

Terah

About the Author

Terah Stearns is a national expert in organizational optimization. With over 25 years of business experience, she has spent the last 16 years helping organizations increase their profitability, build strong process and develop enlightened leadership. As a business consultant and transformational trainer, she has guided over 17 organizations to success.

Stearns has spent years perfecting the techniques shared in *Imagine the Power*. She has given you the questions, the process and the intention that make each of these techniques work *powerfully*.

Stearns has coached hundreds of managers on her enlightened approach which has helped take businesses from pain to profit! *Imagine the Power* is her gift back to a business community that has rewarded her with a lifetime of success.